CHANA

The erudite thoughts of the great scholar, the economist, the strategist and the teacher that serve as DOs Dosn'ts of the everyday life of any person who wants to make his life a grand success

Translation & Comments by :
Vishwamitra Sharma
The English Version
IGEN B.

Manoj Publications

Publishers :

Manoj Publications
761, Main Road, Burari, Delhi-110084
Ph: 27611116, 27611349, Fax : 27611546
Mobile : 9868112194
E-mail : info@manojpublications.com
Website : www.manojpublications.com

Showroom :

Manoj Publications
1583-84, Dariba Kalan, Chandani Chowk,
Delhi-110006
Ph. : 23262174, 23268216, Mob. : 9818753569

Eighteenth Edition : 2014

Printers :

Jai Maya Offset
Jhilmil Industrial Area, Delhi-110095

COMPLETE CHANAKYA NEETI : Vishwamitra Sharma

CHANAKYA NEETI

Chanakya was no beauty in the physical sense. The detractors had no hesitation in proclaiming that he was ugly. But the beauty is only skin deep. Down below he was a solid mass of intellect, brains, creativity, originality, thinking prowess, learning, statesmanship and masterly over-skills in planning and diplomacy, never seen before in one person. His brilliance brought some light to the darkness of the hopeless medieval India.

This digest of his thoughts can prove a complete guide to make one's life successful. It is no idle claim. A common man's ordinary son, with the help and guidance of Chanakya's political wisdom, rose into our country's finest Emperor, Chandra Gupta Maurya. His thoughts are as valid for a common man as they are for a king.

PREFACE

Some people accuse him of being a ruthless political manipulator. But the same tactics are today considered civilised actions as clever diplomatic moves. May be, he was too ahead of the times he existed in. Whatever he did, he did it to safeguard the interests of his motherland which was being ravaged by narrow minded quarrelling chieftans and kings while a foreign invader was subjugating the country. Like a colossus he made the world take notice of India and warned it to treat it respectfully. To add to these talents, he possessed awesome administrative capabilities and economic planning skills.

Medieval India was not a cohesive unit, but a collection of fiefdoms, kingdoms and mini-empires, often quarrelling among themselves. There was one significant vast kingdom situated around the great capital city of Patliputra (Today's Patna) that dwarfed others. This kingdom was very prosperous state and militarily powerful. The name was Magadha.

That was the time when this land faced the real threat of being turn to pieces by an all-conquering marauder named Alexander, The Great. To make matters worse the land was being ravaged by foolish fiefs, petty-minded kings, debauch rulers, unscrupulous leaders and by gross mismanagement or absence of management. Magadha was under the rule of a corrupt tyrant called Raja Mahananda.

Chanak, the father of Chanakya used to live somewhere in the outskirts of a city situated at the border of that kingdom. Raja Mahananda had a large army. He had become a debauch and a ruthless character, a natural degenarated form of an incapable and ineffecient king. The subjects were suffering his arrogance.

The large Magadha Kingdom was infact a mini empire which was a union of small kingdoms and fiefdoms, most of them ruled by minor kings belonging to Nanda dynasty. As a result of the neglect by Mahananda, the bordering states had begun fighting among themselves. In a far off land, an ambitious king named Alexander was preparing to set out on an expedition to conquer the world marching through the armies of Indian kings.

Chanakya had once presented himself in the Court of the the King Dhanananda of Patliputra to seek a chance to serve the kingdom in the capacity befitting his education, learning and wisdom. But the king humiliated him and expelled him for having an ugly face not to be tolerated in the beautiful setting of the royal court. The infuriated Chanakya took a vow to destroy the arrogant dynasty of Nandas. He selected a promising kid of a commoner and took him to the forests. Chanakya brought up the kid as his protege who in course of time rose to vanquish Nanda kings and become Emperor Chandra Gupta. All due to the training, education and guidance by Chanakya in warfare, political manoeuvring, manipulations and strategies. Through cunning diplomacy Chanakya wisely turned the Governor appointed by Alexander into an ally.

He was an able administrator as well. He played lead roles in setting up administrative machinery, policy plannings and in making laws, rules and regulations of the departments. As Kautilya he wrote *'Arthshastra'*, a draft of a constitution of an ideal state.

Due to his political wisdom and diplomatic skills in empire building, Chanakya is called 'Machiaville of India'. But late Prime Minister of India, Jawahar Lal Nehru was of the opinion that the comparison was unfair. He rated Chanakya several times more clever and superior political thinker.

Even after becoming the Emperor, Chandra Gupta

respected Chanakya as his guru and the sole guiding spirit. And for Chanakya, the Emperor Chandra Gupta was a living testimony of his achievements and accomplishments of life.

India has a long tradition of producing great characters in every era who never failed to catch the attention of the world and inspired the human race by giving it a new insight, idea, thought, ideology or a new religion to open up a new path. This fact needs no proof. Chanakya definitely is one of them.

'Chanakya Neeti' is extremely significant book which can guide a person to achieve goals of life and reach new heights of successes. When Chanakya's thoughts can make a common boy into a magnificiant Emperor Chandra Gupta, why can't they benefit you as well? You may not become an emperor literally but you can crown yourself with a successful life—full of achievements. Afterall, a person is a state that has the capacity to become an empire within, an empire of a fulfilled life. So, log on to Chanakya's thoughts.

Every effort has been made to retain the original spirit, meaning and the flavour of the shlokas (couplets or quatrains) in the translation. The language has been kept as simple as possible to make the wisdom of Chanakya, easy to understand for the benefit of all the readers.

❑ ❑

CHAPTER ONE

Do not live in a country that does not allow you; self-respect, honour, means of living, a family, kith and kin, friends, well wishers, ways of education and self-development. Quit such country. It is not fit for living.

प्रणम्य शिरसा विष्णुं त्रैलोक्याधिपतिं प्रभुम् ।
नानाशास्त्रोद्धृतं वक्ष्ये राजनीतिसमुच्चयम् ।।

I bow my head to the Master of the Universe, Almighty and Omnipresent, Lord Vishnu. After paying my obeisance I will venture to present the political knowledge collected from many scriputres.(1)

It has been a tradition of our land that sages and scholars invoked the name of God before beginning any task for the success of the effort. Guru Chanakya prayed to Lord Vishnu before scripting the main matter of this book vide above couplet.

Chanakya has described his work as a fine collection of political wisdom. The same collection is known as *'Chanakya Neeti'* among the common folk.

अधीत्येदं यथाशास्त्रं नरो जानाति सत्तमः।
धर्मोपदेशविख्यातं कार्याऽकार्यं शुभाऽशुभम्।।

After studying this book with due attention, the persons of proper breeding, will learn about what is good and what is bad, according to the wisdom of the great scriptures.(2)

Before embarking on a task one should have the knowledge about its desirability and the consequences. What is proper and what is improper? And only the persons of high upbringing have the capacity to understand the messages contained in the revered scriptures.

One should have proper understanding of lawful and unlawful. For example; normally taking life is murder, a crime and a sinful act. But in certain circumstances the act of murder is not a crime or a sin, like in the battlefield or in self-defence.

तदहं सम्प्रवक्ष्यामि लोकानां हितकाम्यया।
येन विज्ञानमात्रेण सर्वज्ञत्वं प्रपद्यते।।

For the benefit of the common people I will state the political knowledge which makes one wise in all respects. (3)

Chanakya claims that this book shall make any careful reader who has capacity to learn, a real know-all, one whose mind is trained to differentiate instantly the good or bad, the right or wrong and the proper or improper in any given situation. He won't have any confusions about making right decisions.

मूर्खशिष्योपदेशेन दुष्टस्त्रीभरणेन च।
दुःखितैः सम्प्रयोगेण पण्डितोऽप्यवसीदति।।

A wise person will come to grief if he does the unwise acts of; giving advice to a foolish pupil, looking after a woman of loose character and keeping the company of a sad one who has lost his fortune. (4)

According to Chanakya, offering advice to a stupid disciple brings more harm than doing any good. Remember the story about a sparrow and a monkey? A sparrow once advised a foolish monkey who was shivering in the cold to make fire for warmth. The angered monkey killed the sparrow for daring to counsel it. Similarly sheltering a bad woman creates problems and brings infamy to the provider of the shelter.

Anyone who is sad because of loss of money or health is always lamenting and cursing his ill luck. The complaining never ends. One who keeps company to such person also catches the sadness and becomes gloomy. His attitude becomes negative and he begins slipping down in his own work or profession. Besides, listening to the sad one's constant complaints results in terrible loss of time which a wise creative person can ill afford. The person who has sympathetic ears for others often get cheated, tricked into lending money or gets dragged into some misadventure which results in his becoming another sad one.

दुष्टा भार्या शठं मित्रं भृत्यश्चोत्तरदायकः ।
ससर्पे च गृहे वासो मृत्युरेव न संशयः ॥

It is a living death to stay in a house where there is; an evil natured, badmouthing woman of low morals, or a cunning and deceitful friend, or an impolite talkative servant, or a possibility of the presence of a snake. (5)

A house which is the home of an evil woman spells only pain, mental torture, shame and misery for the man who lives there. He is helpless and looks a living tragedy, A deceitful friend is not trustworthy. He will bring disaster any time causing a great grief. An impolite servant upsets his master's mind every now and then. He creates embarrassing situations in the presence of others. He is virtually a threat to the honour of anyone who enters that house. And the presence of a snake is like having death around ready to strike any moment.

आपदर्थे धनं रक्षेद् दारान् रक्षेद्धनैरपि।
आत्मानं सततं रक्षेद् दारैरपि धनैरपि।।

For the bad days one should save money. Woman should be protected even if it takes the money saved. But for self-preservation, the money and the woman should be sacrificed, if required. (6)

It is an accepted fact that money must be saved for hard times. Everyone tries to do so for himself and for his family. A host of saving and Insurance schemes offered by financial institutions are for the very same purpose. But one has the duty to save his woman even by staking all his money because she is one's life partner. Today, the laws say that half of the wealth of a man legally belongs to his wife anyway. In Chanakya's time, however, the laws did not recognise a woman's rights so forcefully. It was merely a moral burden. Chanakya thinks that self-preservation is the foremost duty of a person towards himself. One should do so even at the cost of one's woman. It is basic instict also which applies to animals as well in that sense. In those days, a woman was merely considered an item belonging to a man. Today, the situation is different. Women are accepted as human beings having equal rights as men. But man left to his basic instincts would do what Chanakya has proposed. A natural selection of option.

आपदर्थे धनं रक्षेच्छ्रीमतां कुत आपदः।
कदाचिच्चलिता लक्ष्मीः संचितोऽपि विनश्यति।।

For hard times and to deal with the troubles, a man must protect his wealth because the one who has money, he can overcome hurdles easily. The money, if not protected slips away fast. (7)

Chanakya thinks that a person of wealth can ride over the problems without much difficulty. But the wealth or money is not easy to hold on to. The money is a slippery customer. It does not like to stay at one place and manages to get spent. Even the protected money can get lost because it attracts the attention of unlawful elements.

यस्मिन् देशे न सम्मानो न वृत्तिर्न च बान्धवाः ।
न च विद्याऽऽगमः कश्चित् तं देशं परिवर्जयेत् ।।

Do not live in a country that does not allow you; self-respect, honour, means of living, a family, kith and kin, friends, well wishers, ways of education and self-development. Quit such country. It is not fit for living. (8)

The above facilities are very fundamental for human existence. An land without any one of them can make one's life barren and incomplete in some way or the other. A man needs suitable conditions for his physical, emotional and intellectual survival. Chanakya strongly advises migration from a country that fails to fulfil above conditions essential for an honourable living.

धनिकः श्रोत्रियो राजा नदी वैद्यस्तु पञ्चमः ।
पञ्च यत्र न विद्यन्ते न तत्र दिवसं वसेत् ।।

A man should not make a place his home where there are no; prosperous people, soldiers, scholarly Brahmins, a king, river and physicians. (9)

The presence of wealthy people means the place has flourishing trade and commerce to offer opportunity. Scholarly

Brahmins provide spiritual guidance. A king is a symbol of law and order. The soldiers give a citizen the sense of security from invasions. The river is a source of water which is basic necessity for everyday life and for good harvests. The physicians are needed to ensure good health. All these five things make a citizen's life secure and comfortable and the place worth living.

लोकयात्रा भयं लज्जा दाक्षिण्यं त्यागशीलता।
पञ्च यत्र न विद्यन्ते न कुर्यात् तत्र संस्थितिम्॥

A place that does not offer; means of living, fear of law, feeling of shame for shameless acts, clever people to inspire artful creations and crafts and the spirit of charity, is not fit for living. (10)

These five things are must for a safe, secure, rich and dignified life which every person aspires for. A place that fails these qualifications will be a bad choice to make home at.

जानीयात् प्रेषणे भृत्यान् बान्धवान् व्यसनाऽऽगमे।
मित्रं चाऽऽपत्तिकालेषु भार्यां च विभवक्षये॥

The testing times of the following are as; the wife when the money is gone, the friend in the time of need, the relatives in times of crisis and the servants when they are assigned a mission. In such times they show their true faces. (11)

Guru Chanakya reveals that fidelity of a wife is tested when her husband loses his money. If she is untrue she will desert her husband. A friend in need is the friend indeed. Sincere relatives come to the rescue of their kin in trouble. The trustworthiness of servants is revealed when they are sent out on some mission. Out of the sight of the master, their true nature will surface to show their real identity. A man fallen on bad days sees the true faces of the people around him and learns the shocking truths.

आतुरे व्यसने प्राप्ते दुर्भिक्षे शत्रु-संकटे।
राजद्वारे शमशाने च यस्तिष्ठति स बान्धवः।।

A real brother is one stands by; in the period of grave illness, in times of misfortune, during famines or invasions by enemy, in royal court and in death. He will stick through thick and thin. (12)

In above mentioned situations a man needs someone by his side to draw help or courage from. He will find only the true ones standing by. There will be no sight of the fairwealther friends or hangers on of happy days. During Chanakya days, a person was called to the royal court mostly for unpleasant reasons. The kings were arrogant and arbitrary. Only a person of great courage and conviction could accompany a summoned person to the court which entailed grave risk to himself in the form of the wrath of the king. The other situations illustrated in the couplet by Chanakya hardly need any explanation as they are too simple to be elaborated. The readers should know by their own experience except the one about the death. The simple truth is that only the true one will feel the loss and mourn someone's death. We hope the soul of the departed one sees it.

यो ध्रुवाणि परित्यज्य अध्रुवं परिषेवते।
ध्रुवाणि तस्य नश्यन्ति अध्रुवं नष्टमेव च।।

The one who runs after an uncertain object leaving the certain one, does not get any. He loses the both (13)

It is Chanakya's way of saying that a bird in hand is better two in the bush. And there is a message to be content with whatever you have got. The greed for more brings no good.

वरयेत् कुलजां प्राज्ञो विरूपामपि कन्यकाम्।
रूपवतीं न नीचस्य विवाहः सदृशे कुले।।

*A wise man must marry a girl of high breed even if she
be ugly to look at. He should not fall for a girl of low
upbringing however beauteous she may be. The best course
is to marry in the family of equal status. (14)*

Here, Chanakya has advised a thing of a great common
sense. A girl of low upbringing is more likely to be uneducated,
uncultured and of ill manners. Her foolish behaviour will
cause pain, anguish, embarrassment and humiliation to her
husband of higher status. The beauty will prove of no
consolation. A girl of good upbringing will compensate the
lack of physical beauty with graceful manners and intelligent
talk. She would prove an invaluable asset to her husband in
the long run.

The most sensible thing is to marry in the family of equal
rating. In our society the marital alliance is infact marriage
between two families. Being of the same class and the same
upbringing the members of the families jell together
beautifully without causing any problems. The man and his
wife also fit into the schemes of one another and the life sails
smoothly.

नखीनां च नदीनां च शृङ्गीणां शस्त्रपाणिनाम्।
विश्वासो नैव कर्तव्यः स्त्रीषु राजकुलेषु च।।

*Don't ever trust; the beasts with claws or sharp horns,
rivers, the armed persons, women and the members of the
royal families. (15)*

The beasts with horns or claws are dangerous creatures.
Their basic nature is to attack without warning or at slightest
provocation. One is never safe near such beasts. Rivers are
one of the awesome forces of nature which wreak havoc

when the climate changes its mood. A river can suddenly become a raging flood, it may change its course or spring killers like crocodiles. An armed man also poses danger. He can easily get tempted to use his weapon. And women are famous for their fickle mind. The literature of every society is full of the tales of the treachery and betrayals by women. It should be remembered that the man has always has been prejudiced against the women. It was more so when Chanakya penned down his thoughts. Even today, most men firmly believe that no man should have absolute faith in the loyalty of a woman. Similarly, persons of royal families change colours fast. They consider themselves superior to other human beings. They are powerful and arrogant. And the most dangerous thing about them is that they think, they are above law. Moods, whims and fancies rule their minds. You never know when any such person would turn against anyone just to demonstrate his power. Trusting any person of the royal lineage is very risky and unwise thing.

विषादप्यमृतं ग्राह्ममेध्यादपि काञ्चनम् ।
नीचादप्युत्तमा विद्या स्त्रीरत्नं दुष्कुलादपि ॥

If there is nectar in poison, accept it. If there is precious metal or object in filth, retrieve it. If a low breed man has some good knowledge, wisdom, art or quality, imbibe it. If a woman born to a family of disrepute turns out to be a lady of high qualities, possess such a gem. (16)

Here, Chanakya opines that quality of an end product is what really matters. The origin of a person or a thing is not important. Even what the processes a good product goes through is immaterial. He is very clear that a person of low origin can rise to become a fine gentleman of high rating through training and education. Even the handicap of caste can be overcome. He puts premium on quality, value, knowledge, wisdom and art.

स्त्रीणां द्विगुण आहारो बुद्धिस्तासां चतुर्गुणा।
साहसं षड्गुणं चैव कामोऽष्टगुण उच्यते।।

Compared to males the females; eat twice the amount of food, possess cleverness four times, display courage six times and have hunger for sex eight times. (17)

Chanakya appears to be merely relaying the common beliefs among common folk during those times of deepset prejudice against women. Or is there a hint of sarcasm? The women of course do eat variety of things in small amounts all day long having the leisure time in plenty. For them it is time pass exercise, not an act of satisfying the hunger. In modern times women eat very little for the sake of dieting.

Women are accused of being, fickle minded, treacherous, flitacious and disloyal. Add to them the double-crossing, two-timing, cheating and scheming. All these acts require a fair amount of cunning and cleverness. That will make them smart creatures. The males needed not develop these skills because they lived in a safe world where all the laws, social customs and religious diktats were loaded in their favour. The women had to survive in the male dominated systems. Thus, the cleverness was their only survival weapons.

And all the above clever ploys required a big amount of courage to execute them, considering the enormous risks involved. It was always a matter of life or death. The failures meant death or severe punishments and torture. The women had to have the courage of a gladiator.

The women having the eight times more lust is somewhat debatable. They have more sex desire is understandable as the nature has created them to be mothers which is a direct result of the mating with males. But to say that they are eight times over sex crazy is a bit unfair. The fault lies with males who had been seeing women only as sex objects. They failed to judge women beyond that narrow view, in other roles and in other activities. The males recognised the existence of women only when they were mating with them or were engaged in foreplays or during romantic adventures.

Hence, this statement of Chanakya is merely a reflection of the thinking of the males rather than being his educated thought.

The Summary of the Chapter

Before embarking on a mission, the invokation of God is the expression of one's humility and the acceptance of the reality of his existence being insignificant. So, the need for His blessing and inspiration for the successful completion of the task being undertaken.

In the first chapter, Chanakya has warned against having dealings with some types of harmful and undesirable elements which can cause grief, ill fate, pain, financial loss, physical harm, mental agony, shame and embarrassment.

He has given a very good description of a place or country where one can live. Such worthy place must have some basic qualifications and necessary conditions. The place must have established trade and commerce, employment opportunities, good education system, security, good government, reassuring law and order situation, suitable conditions to raise family, to spawn claws, make friends, to seek spiritual guidance, opportunities to learn arts and crafts, adequate water resources and the presence of noble and charitable people. And above all the place must provide due honour and allow self-respect to its residents.

Chanakya also stresses the need for one to save money for hard times and advocates its protection. He strongly recommends self preservation at every cost.

At a place, he has illustrated the times and situations when others can be tested for their loyalty and sincerety.

As a marriage counselor, he puts premium on the upbringing of the bride, her inner beauty in the form of cultured manners and intelligence. He thinks little of a mere pretty face with boorish manners. According to him, the best choice is marital alliance between a man and a woman of the families of equal status and of the same class. It makes the marriage compatible and smooth going in perfect harmony.

The most important fact that emerges through this chapter is that Chanakya does not hesitate to rise above caste considerations. He indirectly admits that a person of lower caste can rise with education and become a man of letters, arts and high qualities. The advice is to honour and accept such persons without any reservations.

❑❑

CHAPTER TWO

Those parents are worst enemies of their own children; who do not teach them letters and educate them. Because an uneducated person is spurned in the assembly of the learned people. He is total misfit as a crane is in the flock of the stately swans.

अनृतं साहसं माया मूर्खत्वमतिलुब्धता ।
अशौचत्वं निर्दयत्वं स्त्रीणां दोषाः स्वभावजाः ।।

Speaking falsehood, starting a work without giving it any consideration or thought, daredevilry, deceitful behaviour, foolish acts, greed, impurity and cruelty; these are things basic to the nature of the women. (1)

Above traits have been seen in the women from ancient times or they have been so accused of. It is not that the men don't show above weaknesses. They do. But finding faults with women has been favourite passtime of the males. The frailities of the women are more noticeable because their behaviour has always been under the microscope mostly operated by males. In the present age women are becoming educated and the above weaknesses are being washed away. As they are getting shifted to shouldering the more and more serious responsibilities of the society and the administration, their nature too is aquiring depth. The shallowness of uneducated woman is disappearing. Most of the above shortcomings were due to illiteracy and lack of education among women in that bygone era. Today, the scene is changing mercifully.

भोज्यं   भोजनशक्तिश्च   रतिशक्तिर्वराङ्गना।
विभवो दानशक्तिश्च नाऽल्पस्य तपसः फलम्।।

Only great penance can earn one; the rich food to eat, a good digestive power to dispose it, a beautiful woman for wife, and virility to ravish her and riches with charitable disposition to use the money for good causes. (2)

Here we can safely substitute hard work for penance. Hardwork means physical labour which will earn money for buying good food. It will make one hungry and give digestive power as well. Virility will come as a bonus. Getting a beautiful woman would require some good luck, of course. The industriousness should eventually bring riches as its reward. Giving charity will be the icing to the cake. All this is nothing less than a boon earned for a long penance.

यस्य पुत्रो वशीभूतो भार्या छन्दाऽनुगामिनी।
विभवे यश्च सन्तुष्टस्तस्य स्वर्ग इहैव हि।।

This very earth is heaven for one whose; son is obedient, the wife is faithful and whose own heart is content with what money he has got. (3)

Everyone wants to be happy but happiness is elusive. It depends on several factors. The most important factor is domestic peace which is the key to happiness. In case of India it is more true because almost all males here are family men.

It was still more true during Chanakya's time when life was not complicated and a man's life was restricted to the activities of earning livelihood and sustaining his family. Thus, a peaceful home was cause of joy and a family contented with whatever the breadwinner brought was a great relief to him. The conditions mentioned in the couplet by Chanakya ensured the happiness for the man and his family.

ते पुत्रा.ये पितुर्भक्ताः स पिता यस्तु पोषकः।
तन्मित्रं यस्य विश्वासः सा भार्या यत्र निर्वृतिः।।

The true son is one who is obedient to his father, a true father is one who looks after his sons, similarly true friend is one who is trustworthy and true wife is one who makes her husband happy. (4)

As Chanakya said rightly, the obedient sons are like great assets to their father. They can fulfil his dreams and give feeling of security to an aging father.

Unruly sons cause disappointments and anguish to their father. It is father's duty to feed his sons and groom them properly to succeed in life. Everyone understands the worth of a friend who can be trusted. It needs no elaboration. And a wife who makes life happy will be everyman's dream. She can make or mar a man's life. A quarrelsome, disloyal, untrustworthy and selfish wife ruins her man. She holds the key to a man's happiness. And the wife is where the family starts.

परोक्षे कार्यहन्तारं प्रत्यक्षे प्रियवादिनम्।
वर्जयेत्तादृशं मित्रं विषकुम्भं पयोमुखम्।।

A friend who talks flatteringly sweet things overtly but covertly tries to harm should be gotten rid of without any delay. He is like a pot that is filled with poison but is topped with cream to deceive. (5)

A deceitful friend should not be allowed to stay around because he is more dangerous than any of your enemies. He knows your secrets and he has access to your home and your business to be able to do most damage possible. He knows your family and others connected to you, which can help him use them or play some misleading game. Don't ever take chance with such a friend. He is like a bomb tied to your belt. A time bomb waiting to explode when it likes to.

न विश्वसेत् कुमित्रे च मित्रे चाऽपि न विश्वसेत् ।
कदाचित् कुपितं मित्रं सर्व गुह्यं प्रकांशयेत् ।।

A friend who is no good, should not be trusted and a freind who is not proven bad should also be not trusted with your secrets because he might reveal them when he is not on good terms with you. (6)

Chanakya cautions us about friends. There is no question of putting faith in a bad friend. Even good friend should be kept away from your personal and business secrets. You never know what situations the future will throw up. The friend might turn against you due to some reason. He might become your enemy or your rival in love, competition or business. Then the secrets you have told him will become your disadvantages. They can be used against you to harm your interests. This advice of Chanakya is more valid in today's world where relationships have become extremely instable. The people keep changing friends like they change clothes. Keep your secrets to yourself.

मनसा चिन्तितं कार्यं वाचा नैव प्रकाशयेत् ।
मन्त्रेण रक्षयेद् गूढं कार्ये चाऽपि नियोजयेत् ।।

What plan you have thought of in your mind should not

come on your tongue. Contemplate and rethink over it, keeping it guarded. Put the idea or plan into action without voicing it. (7)

Here Chanakya again emphasizes the need to keep even plans of your projects guarded as secrets. Announcing your plans to all and sundry can be harmful. The failure to execute the plan shall make you a laughing stock of the others. Then there is danger of someone stealing your idea and putting it into action leaving you frustrated and cheated. Revealing the plan shall invite suggestions and criticisms on it which can dampen your spirits. That will weaken your commitment to your plan and it might fail due to lack of your full support. In this regard you must see how today's industries guard their plans, projects, blue prints, designs and new ideas by employing armies of security personnel.

कष्टं च खलु मूर्खत्वं कष्टं च खलु यौवनम् ।
कष्टात्कष्टतरं चैव परगेहनिवासनम् ।।

Stupidity is a woe, the youthful days are woeful, but living on other's mercy is woe extreme. (8)

The stupidity gets only contempt and ridicule of others which is painful. The youthful days make one do rash things and as a result one has to reap a harvest of woes, problems and agonies. Living in another person's house and living on his mercy is painful to the extreme. The honour is gone and the self respect is lost. It is infact a living death.

शैले शैले न माणिक्यं मौक्तिकं न गजे गजे ।
साधवो न हि सर्वत्र चन्दनं न वने वने ।।

Every hill does not contain gems, every elephant has no mani-pearl in its forehead, every place is no home of nobles and every forest does not grow sandalwood trees. (9)

Chanakya says that rare things are found in only rare places. Every place is not blessed with them. Here we would like to offer explanation about the mani-pearl. It is supposed to be a red pearl. According to the mythological belief, a superior heavenly order of elephants are supposed to develop this precious gem inside their foreheads which can be retrieved after the death of the animal. However no specimen of this mani-pearl exists anywhere to support the theory.

पुत्राश्च विविधैः शीलैर्नियोज्याः सततं बुधैः ।
नीतिज्ञाः शीलसम्पन्ना भवन्ति कुलपूजिताः ।।

The wise persons should groom their children carefully to make them persons of high qualities and see them employed in productive work. Only the persons of learning and qualities find respect in the society. (10)

Here Chanakya counsels the well grooming of the offspring. They must be brought up in good health. Education and cultured manners be seeded in them to have them grow into the persons of high learning and fine qualities. It is equally important to see them employed in gainful activity. An idle young person is worthless even if he has qualities. He should not be burden on anyone. In the final analysis a man's real wisdom is reflected in the way his children shape up.

माता शत्रुः पिता वैरी येन बालो न पाठितः ।
न शोभते सभामध्ये हंसमध्ये बको यथा ।।

Those parents are worst enemies of their children; who do not teach them letters and educate them. Because an uneducated person is spurned in the assembly of the learned people. He is total misfit as a crane is in the flock of stately swans. (11)

Chanakya knew the importance of education in life. This fact is so real that all the nations of the present day world have made education a fundamental right in their constitutions. This shows how far ahead in time Chanakya was.

The education is the most correct way of cultivating wisdom in a young mind. An educated person knows about the world around him better and he can conduct his life in a clever manner. He can deal with others smoothly. And it is not easy for others to trick a man of education. In gatherings, an uneducated person is quickly spotted by his silly talk. Such persons curse their parents all their lives.

लालनाद् बहवो दोषास्ताडनाद् बहवो गुणाः।
तस्मात्पुत्रं च शिष्यं च ताडयेन्न तु लालयेत्।।

Too much indulgence spoils a child. Rebuke and cane helps in the development of the child. So, the children and the students must be kept straight through use of stick and rebuke. Don't indulge them. (12)

Children do need love and encouragement. The modern theory is that the stick must be very sparingly used. Some educationists are totally against it. The use of rebuke is also not favoured these days. But perhaps, the situation was different during the period of Chanakya because educational aids were not there. There were no TV, video, newspapers, magazines, books of every kind and toys etc. Today everything around us is education oriented. In absence of all these it was necessary to use rod to induce child to study. Even today parents use the above methods to control their children and generally it works, justifying what Chanakya has said.

श्लोकेन वा तदर्धेन पादेनैकाक्षरेण वा।
अबन्ध्यं दिवसं कुर्याद् दानाध्ययन कर्मभिः।।

A man must read and study a Shloka (sanskrit couplet) everyday. If it is not possible, read half of it, or a part of it or atleast a word. Never let any day go without some study of a written word. One should make his day fruitful by doing good work and study. (13)

Chanakya is indirectly pointing at the importance of learning. A written word is a symbol of education. The message is to keep in touch with education always. Let it inspire you to move towards good things, good work and good thinking. The knowledge is power.

कान्तावियोगः स्वजनापमानः ऋणस्य शेषः कुनृपस्य सेवा।
दरिद्रभावो विषमा सभा च विनाग्निनैते प्रदहन्ति कायम्।।

The following things burn a man without fire and silently eat him; the separation from wife, contempt by kith and kin, serving an evil master, indebtedness, poverty and living amongst selfish and rogue people. (14)

Pining for woman eats a man's heart away like rust eats iron. The insult by near relatives is the ultimate humiliation that causes great auguish. Serving an evil master only earns rebukes and curses. The poverty and being in debt keep one in constant worry. It is like being on slow burner all the time. And selfish and rogue persons mean never ending harassment. Their evil intentions always hang over one's head like Democle's sword. Here, Chanakya is right on every count. Above conditions silently keep corroding a man's heart, soul and body from within.

नदीतीरे च ये वृक्षाः परगेहेषु कामिनी।
मन्त्रिहीनाश्च राजानः शीघ्रं नश्यन्त्यसंशयम्।।

The following take no time to perish; the trees growing on a river bank, a woman who lives in other man's house and a king who has bad ministers. (15)

The trees growing on a river bank live perilously. The day, the river is flooded, the trees will get washed away uprooted. A woman living in another man's house is always in danger of getting dishonoured and abused. Even if it does not happen, she will not be acceptable to her real man anyway. She faces ruin. A king with bad ministers will ruin his kingdom through mismanagement, corruption and treachery. The king himself is not safe with such ministers around.

बलं विद्या च विप्राणां राज्ञां सैन्यं बलं तथा।
बल वित्तं च वैश्यानां शूद्राणां परिचर्यकम्।।

The power of Brahmins is their knowledge, the power of kings is their armies, the power of traders is their money and the power of the lower classes is their service. (16)

Chanakya has often referred to Brahmins as being synonymous with the scholars or men of knowledge. The reason is obvious. The priesthood being the main occupation of Brahmins, they were required to learn the letters to be able to read the scriptures and to write birth rolls (Janmapatris). But merely knowing to read and write does not make one a scholar. Most of them were literate without doubt, for survival, but not men of learning. The warrior castes and traders were not interested in scholarly pursuits. Education was denied to lower castes.

Thus, the Brahmins had monopoly over education facilities. As a result all of them were generally taken for learned people by others. Thus, by Brahmin Chanakya really means a scholar by default or scholars who happen to be Brahmins.

The lower casts did labour work or various manual jobs providing services to the other upper casts who considered such work not fit for their status. Thus, for services the upper casts were dependent on the lower castes conceding them some bargaining power.

निर्धनं पुरुषं वेश्या प्रजा भग्नं नृपं त्यजेत् ।
खगा वीतफलं वृक्षं भुक्त्वा चाऽभ्यागता गृहम् ।।

A prostitute deserts impoverished customer, subjects desert a vanquished king, birds desert trees that have ceased to bear fruits and a surprise guest leaves quickly after partaking food. (17)

Of course, a prostitute has no use for a moneyless customer. Charity is not her nature. A defeated king loses the respect and trust of his subjects. The birds prefer to live on the trees that provide them with food in the form of fruits. A surprise guest leaves quickly because he does not want to tax his kind hosts any more. Appearance of a surprise guest upsets the plans and the rhythm of the hosts. His departure restores the normalcy in the house. It is the guest's civilised gesture. One should know when to get up and go. That saves one's honour and embarrassing situation. The people or things come together with some definite purpose or for mutual benefit. It is time to break up when a factor arises which makes that purpose or benefit not possible.

गृहीत्वा दक्षिणां विप्रास्त्यजन्ति यजमानकम् ।
प्राप्तविद्या गुरुं शिष्या दग्धाऽरण्यं मृगास्तथा ।।

Brahmins leave the houses of their clients soon after receiving alms. The pupil leave the place of their guru after completing the education and the creatures of the forest run away from it when the forest is on fire. (18)

It should be the way of the things, Chanakya hints here. There is no use of one lingering at a place where the task is finished. It is proper to depart after completion of a mission. Those who stay back aimlessly lose the respect of others because his unwanted presence creates discomfort for others and upsets their programmes. Others can have some other business to deal with which may be being delayed due to their lingerer on. After the party is over the guests leave one by one. The hosts don't like the persons who delay their departure on some pretext or other and keep forcing their presence longer and longer. Sometimes hosts have to remind such guests in a polite way that he must leave. May be, the hosts won't invite them next time.

दुराचारी दुरदृष्टिर्दुराऽऽवासी च दुर्जनः ।
यन्मैत्री क्रियते पुम्भिर्नरः शीघ्रं विनश्यति ॥

One who befriends a person of bad character, a person of bad intentions, a person who is a sinner or a person who lives at an evil place; gets destroyed in quick time. (19)

Besides Chanakya, all other moral teachers also agree that keeping a bad company leads to ruin. One should keep away from such characters for one's own good. The evil will rub off to the person who associates himself with them. The people will take him for one of the rogues.

समाने शोभते प्रीतिः राज्ञि सेवा च शोभते ।
वाणिज्यं व्यवहारेषु दिव्या स्त्री शोभते गृहे ॥

The friendship is proper between two people of the same rank or social status, the best job is to be in the service of the king, trading is the best occupation and a pretty woman is the most graceful in the home setting. (20)

The friendship between equals is the most natural and compatible. There is no clash of egoes and the respect is mutual. They don't look odd to the eyes of the others. Unmatched friendship often becomes target of snide remarks and suspecions which creates bad feelings. The best job is that which offers stability. In middle ages serving the king was the only stable employment and it commanded respect in the society. The business of trading is risky but it offers good profits and the surest way to get rich. The best thing about it is that a trader is a free person, master of his own life.

A pretty woman is most safe and secure in a home. For such woman outside world could be dangerous and full of traps.

The Summary of the Chapter

In this chapter Chanakya has been a bit uncharitable to the woman-kind. But his thoughts can be justified since they were formed in a different age and in different conditions when prejudicies ruled the societies.

There is a lot of comments and advices on family relationships. A great emphasis has been laid on the education of the children as a parental duty. Obedient sons and faithful wives have been given due credit as the joys of a man's life. He has made caustic remarks against the parents who do not care to groom their offsprings through education. Use of rod and rebuke have been suggested as good methods for making the children learn things. It may not go well with modern educationists who think otherwise.

Everyone has been advised to read something everyday to keep in touch with the learning. He also explains the improperiety of lingering at a place without any purpose. One should know when to leave gracefully because overstaying makes one's presence unwelcome and it invites contempt of others.

People have been asked to stay away from bad company. The compatibility of a friendship and good occupations also get Chanakya's mention. According to him the trading is the best profession.

One more important advice is that one should not reveal one's ideas or plans to others. Even friends should not be confided with all the personal secrets.

❑ ❑

CHAPTER THREE

If you were to choose between evil person and a snake to keep company with, opt for the snake. Because a snake will bite only in self-defence but an evil person can put a bite for any reason and any time or always.

कस्य दोषः कुले नास्ति व्याधिना को न पीडितः।
व्यसनं केन न प्राप्तं कस्य सौख्यं निरन्तरम्।।

Which family is there in this world that has no blemish? Which person is there who has never fallen ill? Who has not ever been in trouble due to some bad habit? Who has always been happy? (1)

In this world nothing is perfect. The life is a mixture of good and bad. The day is followed by night. Happiness is not forever. There is something wrong with everything and everyone. Everyone has made some mistake one time or other. Chanakya is trying to convey the message that we should not find fault with others. No one should be condemned for some minor flaw or mistake. Because it is nature's law for everything to be imperfect.

31

आचारः कुलमाख्याति देशमाख्याति भाषणम्।
सम्भ्रमः स्नेहमाख्याति वपुराख्याति भोजनम्।।

A man's behaviour shows his class, a man's language reveals his native place, a persons hospitality betrays his affection and a person's bulk tells about his food intake. (2)

Manners of a person clearly demonstrate his upbringing, the class of his family. The language of a person or his accent gives clear indication of the place he comes from. An infatuated person can't hide his joy or excitement while greeting the loved one. And of course, a man's size is an advertisement of his diet, the quantity of the food he consumes.

सुकुले योजयेत्कन्यां पुत्रं विद्यासु योजयेत्।
व्यसने योजयेच्छत्रुं मित्रं धर्मे नियोजयेत्।।

A wise man's duty is; to marry his daughter in high family, to give high education to sons, to introduce the enemy to some fatal addiction and to get his friend engaged in some noble task. (3)

Marrying daughter in high family ensures her happiness. The girls in our society are not masters of their own destiny. Her happiness depends on the attitudes of the members of her husband's family. She will need the help of good, cultured and kind members of that family to get adjusted and accepted. And then, high families are mostly prosperous which will make her life comfortable.

Sons, with high education can make good careers and succeed in life. And Chanakya's suggestion of introducing the enemy to some ruinous addiction is interesting. Today we see this trick being played all around us. Many nations are engaged in secretly spreading drug addiction among the youth of the enemy countries. The money earned through drug sales is being used to finance terrorism to make matters worse. In most of the countries drug menance is playing havoc. Our own country is one of the major victims.

दुर्जनस्य च सर्पस्य वरं सर्पो न दुर्जनः।
सर्पो दंशति कालेन दुर्जनस्तु पदे पदे।।

If you were to choose between an evil person and a snake to keep company with, opt for the snake. Because the snake will bite you only in self-defence but the evil person will put a bite for any reason and any time or always. (4)

An evil persons posses greater danger than a snake. A snake might turn out to be a poisonless type. But never so with an evil person. He is nothing but poison. A snake attacks only when it feels threatened but for an evil person biting is a game, a natural exercise like breathing or blinking. Never ever trust an evil person, is Chanakya's sincere advice.

एतदर्थं कुलीनानां नृपाः कुर्वन्ति संग्रहम्।
आदिमध्याऽवसानेषु न त्यजन्ति च ते नृपम्।।

The wise kings always keep the persons of noble lineage around them because they always stand by them, be it the time of ascendence or period of descendence or the time of troubles. (5)

The persons of noble lineage are blessed with stable characters and their grooming makes them wise, learned and of high qualities. Such people are the strength of the king, a great help in running the state. Loyalty and steadfastness is basic qualities of their character. The king can depend on them in all kinds of times and situations. Even in defeat the nobles don't desert the king. Many kings make a come back with the help of their loyal nobles. The history is replete with such examples. One other reason why nobles show such solidarity with the king is that their own future and fate lies in his continuation as the sovereign of the land.

प्रलये भिन्नमर्यादा भवन्ति किल सागराः।
सागरा भेदमिच्छन्ति प्रलयेऽपि न साधवः।।

In dooms' day conditions even seas cross their limits and submerge the land but noble characters have more depth than even the seas. At no time they cross their limits in whatever the conditions of troubles and calamities. (6)

Here Chanakya is paying eloquent tribute to the exemplary characters of men of substance, high breed and of noble education. No provocation, no amount of anger and no crisis can make such people lose their cool. They always retain their dignity and their principles. In no circumstance do they fail to honour commitments.

मूर्खस्तु परिहर्तव्यः प्रत्यक्षो द्विपदः पशुः।
भिनत्ति वाक्शल्येन अदृष्टः कण्टको यथा।।

A stupid person physically looks just like any other human being inspite of being an ass and he is no better than an animal still. He is pain in the neck of a wise person like an embedded thorn. (7)

An uneducated person is pain. His foolish talk hits a wise one like whiplash. His foolish behaviour causes great anguish like a thorn does when it goes deep down in the flesh. Chanakya equates an uneducated foolish persons with an animal. Presence of such person around was simply intolerable to him. Everything about a fool aroused his anger. It simply shows how deeply he valued the education.

रूपयौवनसम्पन्नाः   विशालकुलसम्भवाः।
विद्याहीना न शोभन्ते निर्गन्धा इव किंशुकाः।।

A young person with handsome face, brimming with

energy and born to a high family, if uneducated, attracts no admirers, like a scentless flower he is ignored. (8)

Here Chanakya again betrays his deep felt empathy to creed and caste. He puts prime value on education. A person born to a high family of high caste is no better than a lowly animal if he is not educated. Education is the best medicine for ignorance, shallowness, cheapness and stupidity. Scentless flowers wither without attracting bees or insects or admiring humans. Similarly a man's caste, blood line and physical beauty becomes irrelevant if he has no education.

कोकिलानां स्वरो रूपं स्त्रीणां रूपं पतिव्रतम् ।
विद्या रूपं कुरूपाणां क्षमा रूपं तपस्विनाम् ।।

The beauty of a Cuckoo is in its call, the sweetness and the beauty of a woman lies in her piety, the beauty of an ugly one is in his learning and the beauty of the sages is in their kindness. (9)

The real beauty of a thing is not in its physical shape but in its qualities. A cuckoo is admired by all because of her sweet call although it looks like a crow. A woman of no character gets no respects however beauteous she may be. Only snide remarks chase her. An ugly person wins others with his inner beauty of wisdom and superior character. And the beauty of great people, sages and the high and mighty is in displaying kindness. Because a person who has risen high holds commonfolk in awe who appreciate kindness. It puts them at ease.

त्यजेदेकं कुलस्यार्थे ग्रामस्यार्थे कुलं त्यजेत् ।
ग्रामं जनपदस्यार्थे आत्मार्थे पृथिवीं त्यजेत् ।।

If a man's expulsion means peace and good of the rest of the clan, then the person must be expelled. If degradation of a village means upliftment of the rest of the district, then it must be done. Similarly for the salvation of the soul, one should not hesitate to depart from this world. (10)

The gist of this couplet is that if some small sacrifice does the larger good, it should be done. The aim should be to achieve the largest good for the largest number of people. If a rupee can be gained by throwing away a paisa, it will be a good bargain. In doing so technicalities and moral issues must not be allowed to stand as hurdles. It is a simple and practical matter of mathematics.

उद्योगे नास्ति दारिद्रचं जपतो नास्ति पातकम् ।
मौने च कलहो नास्ति नास्ति जागरिते भयम् ।।

An industrious person can never be poor, always keeping God in mind keeps one away from sin, the silence does not let quarrels appear and an ever vigilant person has no cause for fear. (11)

Here Chanakya merely reaffirms already accepted facts. A hardworking person is sure to make money. The fear of God saves one from becoming sinful. Silence is another name of tolerance, a guarantee of peace. The tongue is the greatest war-monger. All the quarrels, fights, battles, crimes and wars are indirect products of the things said by tongue. Shut it in its traps and let the silence prevail to live in peace. Eternal vigilance is the price of freedom and freedom from fear.

अतिरूपेण वै सीता अतिगर्वेण रावणः ।
अतिदानात् बलिर्बद्धो अति सर्वत्र वर्जयेत् ।।

Too much beauty got Sita kidnapped, too much ego got Ravana killed and too much charity got Raja Bali in deep trouble. Too much of anything is bad. Stay away from too much. (12)

Chanakya's message is clear in the couplet itself. The examples quoted by him are from the epic tale of Ramayana. We all know the story of Rama, Sita and Ravana. Some reader might not have read the tale of Raja Bali. So, here it is:

Raja Bali was a mighty king of demons. He was famous for his charity and generosity. This made him popular and adored all over the universe. People everywhere started singing his praises. This worried the Lords of the heaven who were rivals of demons (Rakshashas). They all trooped to Lord Vishnu and prayed Him to do something before the Raja Bali displaced all Lords and angels from the heaven by the growing power of his deeds of charity. Lord Vishnu transformed himself into a pigmy Brahmin and presented himself before Raja Bali at a certain hour during which the generous Raja gave anything a Brahmin asked for. Raja Bali asked, "Well dear little Brahmin, what do you want?"

"Just the land my three steps can cover, O Mighty Raja." the pigmy humbly begged.

Bali was amused, how much land three pigmy steps could cover? The Guru of demons, Shukracharya sensed some trick and warned Raja Bali. But the king ignored his advice and asked the pigmy to take the steps.

The pigmy alias Lord Vishnu covered the entire universe in three steps and turned Raja Bali a beggar who was left with nothing.

को हि भारः समर्थानां किं दूरं व्यवसायिनाम्।
को विदेशः सविद्यानां कः परः प्रियवादिनाम्।।

Nothing is impossible for powerful and mighty, no place is out of reach for traders, no land is alien for men of learning and no one is stranger for a polite talker. (13)

The powerful and mighty can do whatever they like. Even law bends itself to accommodate their wish. They can overrule everyone else. In the present day world, a person having money power also is all-capable. Traders go to any corner of the world to do their business. Even in middle ages the mindset of the traders was global. They crossed the seas to do trade. Today the entire world economy has become global. And for scholars, learned people and the professionals no country is alien. Wherever they go, they are welcome with open arms and made to feel at home. A strange fact is that Indian scholars get more respect and more recognition abroad. As a result a vast numbers of Indian writers, artists, doctors, engineers and others have virtually made foreign countries their home. And a man who talks politely is darling of all. Even strangers endear him. Very wise observations by Chanakya.

एकेनाऽपि सुवृक्षेण पुष्पितेन सुगन्धिना।
वासितं तद्वनं सर्वं सुपुत्रेण कुलं तथा।।

A single tree laden with sweet scented flowers spreads its fragrance throught the forest. Similarly a worthy son born to a family brings glory to the entire clan or dynasty besides the immediate family. (14)

Chanakya feels that it does not need armies of sons or cousins to do great things. Just one worthy son can redeem entire dynasty and clan. In the warmth of his achievements all the members of the clan can bask. The quality matters, and not the numbers.

एकेन शुष्कवृक्षेण दह्यमानेन वह्निना।
दह्यते तद्वनं सर्वं कुपुत्रेण कुलं तथा।।

A dried tree catches fire and it engulfs the entire forest in flames. Similarly a bad son born to a family can destroy the entire clan. (15)

A bad son is just the antithesis of the worthy son. His misdeeds tarnished the good name earned by the dynasty's earlier men. The entire clan is put to shame. All the honour and the respect of others for the family gets washed away beside causing mental pain, agony and disappointment to the family members.

एकेनाऽपि सुपुत्रेण विद्यायुक्तेन साधुना।
आह्लादितं कुलं सर्वं यथा चन्द्रेण शर्वरी।।

If the only son comes good as a scholar gentleman the family is lit up with joy, just like rising of the single moon spreads light into darkness. (16)

An achiever son is the pride of the family who makes all his kith and kin happy. The chests of the family members swell with pride. Mention of his name brings respect to everyone connected with him in any way. Being related to him serves as a testimonial of some worthiness, a passport to honour and acceptability. His is not only a source of joy but an inspiration for other too. A real pride and joy of the parents.

किं जातैर्बहुभिः पुत्रैः शोकसन्तापकारकैः।
वरमेकः कुलाऽऽलम्बी यत्र विश्राम्यते कुलम्।।

What is the use of siring good for nothing sons who only bring pain and sorrow? One son who takes care of the family is enough. The who family is happy and safe with him. (17)

Here Chanakya has again laid stress on the good son and criticised the rogue sons. It merely shows the structure and functioning of the family system then. Hopes of the entire family and the clan were centred only on one person, the son. On him fell the sole burden of doing something, to earn name for the family, to feed and look after the entire family, to realise the dreams of the parents and to make everyone happy. The son used to be the sole earning member of the family. Hence, the fate of all the members of the family depend on him. Everyone wanted him to be a success. His failure meant disaster for the family and the grim old age for the parents. The sons were under relentless pressure to succeed for the survival of the family. Some sons cracked under this pressure and were doomed to fail. This set up was somewhat unhealthy. And it continues to be so in most of the families although today more members of the family work and earn money. But the main pressure is still on the son.

You can guess why Chanakya is talking of the importance of the worthy son again and again.

लालयेत् पञ्च वर्षाणि दश वर्षाणि ताडयेत्।
प्राप्ते तु षोडशे वर्षे पुत्रं मित्रवदाचरेत्।।

Indulge son upto the fifth year of his age, cane and rebuke can be used for the next ten years. But when he enters 16th year of his age, then on he must be treated as a friend by the father.(18)

We have already commented on the stick and rebuke advice of Chanakya. The last part of his advice is very sensible and modern. Most of the educated parents today treat their children as their friends and live happily. It does not spoil the children. Many parents start treating their children as friends even before their 16th year. Some foolish parents go on treating their sons as children even when they have grown adults. It stunts the mental growth of the son. And sometimes the adult son feels greatly embarrassed when he is rebuked like a child infront of others. This thing is more common in Indian families. Such foolish parents excuse themselves by saying that the children always remain children in the eyes of the parents.

40

उपसर्गेऽन्यचक्रे च दुर्भिक्षे च भयावहे।
असाधुजनसम्पर्के यः पलायति स जीवति।।

In face of calamities like, excess rains, draught, riots, breaking out of some epidemic, external invasion, acute famine and the sight of evil people; one who runs away saves his life. (19)

Advice here is not to be fool hardy. When there is some calamity about which you can do nothing, you should flee. Don't stay there to be destroyed. Remember that the discretion is the better part of valour. Here, note that Chanakya has treated the presence of evil people as nothing less than a natural calamity.

धर्मार्थकाममोक्षाणां यस्यैकोऽपि न विद्यते।
जन्म-जन्मनि मर्त्येषु मरणं तस्य केवलम्।।

A person who has no faith, no wealth, no love and no salvation, goes on taking birth and dying without any purpose. (20)

Here faith stands for religion. Religion instils in one the basic values of life, the desire to do right things and to stick to the moral codes and ethics. In old times religion was the only guide to the moral values.

A man having earned wealth means he has made a material success of his life. He can make merry and enjoy all the good things of life.

Love is a blessing in itself. It gives one a family, children and life long work of looking after his family. He too gains something in life, a mission to complete making the life purposeful.

Salvation comes through noble deeds, charity, penance and meditation. At least the after life will be secure.

One who has done none of the above acts has perhaps

idled away his life. He has done nothing, achieved nothing, enjoyed nothing and there is nothing to look forward to even after death.

मूर्खा यत्र न पूज्यन्ते धान्यं यत्र सुसञ्चितम्।
दम्पत्येः कलहो नास्ति तत्र श्रीः स्वयमागता॥

Where stupid people are not honoured, where food-grains are stored safely and where man and woman do not quarrel; in such place descends Laxmi, the goddess of prosperity and wealth. (21)

The only place where stupid are not honoured can be a state where wisdom rules. The wise people in charge means a well governed and well managed state which will naturally be prosperous. The food will always be available because it is stored. The peace between man and woman means harmonious families and peaceful homes. It is only possible in good economic conditions and in everyone being happy and satisfied. In hard times people quarrel. All the above conditions lead to a state that is prosperous with everyone around happy.

The Summary of the Chapter

In this chapter the great Guru says that we must overlook minor defects in others. Nothing is perfect. He has worked out an interesting way to destroy the enemy. That is by introducing him to addiction.

If you were to see an evil person and a snake, the wise thing is to kill the evil man first. He is more harmful.

Chanakya has compared an uneducated fool with an animal. He feels that a person of good lineage and of physical beauty is worthless if he is uneducated.

Worthy sons of the family have been praised sky high as

they have realised the hopes of the parents and brought joy to the family. The failed and good for nothing sons have been castigated. It is because the survival of the entire family depends on the success of the son. We can detect the amount of pressure everyone puts on the son. He is supposed to get educated and start earning to support the family as soon as possible, at the same time get married and breed children besides keeping on learning and becoming a scholar. Something fit for a superman. But that is how our society is. One person carries the entire burden of the family.

The best piece of Chanakya's tip in this chapter is for the parents to treat their 15 year plus old children as friends.

There is advice for working for the larger good even at the cost of a minor loss or sacrifice. He has illustrated how too much of everything is bad. The global attitudes of scholars and traders have also been pointed at.

If a person is not religious, or not rich, or not in love or has no family, or has no credit of good deeds for the deliverance of the soul, then, Chanakya declares that such person has wasted his life and shamed his birth.

❑❑

CHAPTER FOUR

A man must quit a religion that does not preach love and kindness, a man must leave a teacher who has little knowledge, a man must leave a woman who has foul temper and a man must break off with kith and kin who have no love for him.

आयुः कर्म च वित्तं च विद्या निधनमेव च।
पञ्चैतानि हि सृज्यन्ते गर्भस्थस्यैव देहिनः।।

When a life gets seeded in a mother's womb, its age, deeds, wealth, education and death, all are determined right there. (1)

Here Chanakya seems to believe that everything about a persons life is predetermined at the very time of conception. Call it fate or *kismet*. Sometimes this belief in fate makes our ancient scholars contradict themselves. If everything is predetermined then all the advices contained in these chapters become redundant.

Hence, we must presume that the predetermined fate is things that have been granted. But nevertheless, a person will have to struggle, make effort and go through all the rigours of life to realise those grants practically. Otherwise the grants lapse. In case of failures, a person can draw consolation from the belief that he was not fated to succeed.

साधुभ्यस्ते निवर्तन्ते पुत्रा मित्राणि बान्धवाः ।
ये च तैः सह गन्तारस्तद्धर्मात्सुकृतं कुलम् ।।

Sons, friends, kith and kin can take your mind away from the sermons of noble and holy people you are supposed to be listening to when in their congregations. But don't let your mind wander away from the holy sermons. Their teachings will bless you, your family and other dear ones with goodness. (2)

Chanakya advises that you shouldn't let the thoughts of your near and dear ones distract you when you are listening to the sermons of the holy people. Because your learning something from the sermons will eventually benefit your near and dear ones.

दर्शनध्यानसंस्पर्शैर्मत्सी कूर्मी च पक्षिणी ।
शिशुं पालयते नित्यं तथा सज्जनसंगतिः ।।

Female fish, tortoise and hen birds care their offspring by looking adoringly, by caressing and by pecking gently. Similarly noble saints look after the spiritual needs of the common man through discourses. (3)

In Chanakya's days attending the discourses of the holy men was the only way of getting the spiritual guidance. Today, the scene is different. These holy messages are available as information technology products in the open market can be viewed or heard on TV, Videos and audio cassettes.

यावत्स्वस्थो ह्ययं देहो यावन्मृत्युश्च दूरतः ।
तावदात्महितं कुर्यात् प्राणान्ते किं करिष्यति ।।

While the body is healthy and work-worthy and death is away, one must do charity and good deeds. When the death comes there will be no time left to do anything. (4)

When the body is healthy, the death looks a far away impossible thing. That is an illusion. The death is always hovering around. It would prick the bubble of your life any time and finish your story. So, don't waste time. Now is the time to do whatever good things you always wanted to do. Tomorrow will be too late, warns Chanakya.

कामधेनुगुणा विद्या ह्यकाले फलदायिनी।
प्रवासे मातृसदृशी विद्या गुप्तं धनं स्मृतम्।।

The knowledge is like a holy Kamadhenu cow. It bears fruit in all seasons. In foreign lands it protects and rewards. That is why it is considered inbuilt secret treasure. (5)

Kamdhenu is the fabled mythological cow believed to give out endless streams of milk and fulfil wishes. The knowledge can earn rewards any time. In foreign lands it works like a magic wand in bringing honour, respect and money. A scholar becomes guest of honour anywhere. And acceptability comes readily. He is welcome in any country. It's truly a secret treasure chest.

Today, in IITs foreign companies book brilliant students in advance to serve in their companies or for further studies as soon as they complete education here. We live in a modern world where education is basically technical knowledge oriented.

वरमेको गुणी पुत्रो निर्गुणैश्च शतैरपि।
एकश्चन्द्रस्तमो हन्ति न च ताराः सहस्रशः।।

It is better to have one good son instead of having hundred worthless sons. There are thousands of stars in the sky but it takes a moon to brighten up the world. (6)

No Comment required.

मूर्खश्चिरायुर्जातोऽपि तस्माज्जातमृतो वरः।
मृतः स चाऽल्पदुःखाय यावज्जीवं जडो दहेत्।।

A son dead soon after birth is preferable to an idiot son with a long life. The dead son causes grief once for a brief period. But the living idiot is a life long grief. (7)

An idiot is pain in the neck. If that happens to be the son, then the pain becomes a river of sorrow with a life long course.

कुग्रामवासः कुलहीनसेवा कुभोजनं क्रोधमुखी च भार्या।
पुत्रश्च मूर्खो विधवा च कन्या विनाऽग्निना षट् प्रदहन्ति कायम्।।

The following six things are living funeral for a man; to live in a village of bad characters, to work for an evil family, to get bad food to eat, a short tempered wife, a foolish son and a widowed daughter. (8)

Life and honour will always be in danger for one who unfortunately has to live in a village inhabited by bad characters. He will have sleepless nights. Working for an evil family means getting insulted and harangued constantly. Bad food will give pain and bad health. A foolish son is a life long sorrow. And a widowed daughter is the greatest tragedy that could befall one. Her ruined life and her grief will be unbearable pain for the parents. This pain will increase manifold when the people would taunt and talk bad about her in a narrow minded and orthodex society like ours'.

All the above things can burn a person without fire and turn him into ashes.

किं तया क्रियते धेन्वा या न दोग्ध्री न गर्भिणी।
कोऽर्थः पुत्रेण जातेन यो न विद्वान् न भक्तिमान्।।

What is the use of a barren cow that can't give milk?
What is the use of giving birth to a son who neither is a
scholar nor devoted? (9)

A son becoming a scholar would bring good name to the
family and please his parents. He will also earn some money
and respect too. Thus, a scholar son would become pride of
the family. If he fails to become a scholar, he can still be
useful to his parents by becoming devoted to them. He can
look after them and make them comfortable atleast physically.
That will give enough satisfaction to the parents. It should be
kept in mind that in our system parents are totally dependent
on their sons in old age.

संसार तापदग्धानां त्रयो विश्रान्तिहेतवः।
अपत्यं च कलत्रं च सतां संगतिरेव च।।

In this world, the hot hell of miseries, only three thing
provide some cool relief; good offspring, devoted wife and
the company of noble people. (10)

Life of a common man in those days was very tough.
There was never ending poverty, exploitation, bad kings,
cruel governors, caste systems, robbers, thugs, foreign
invaders, misadministration and instability. In such world for
one, home and family provided some relief. Everyday the
bread winner returned home beaten, tired and worked to
bones. Any one having good children, loving wife and peace
at home found great consolation in them. It helped him
recover and ready himself for the next day's grind.

And sometimes he needed to listen to the sermons of the
holy men to fill his mind's intellectual and spiritual void.
That completed the circle of his narrowed down life.

सकृज्जल्पन्ति राजानः सकृज्जल्पन्ति पण्डिताः।
सकृत् कन्याः प्रदीयन्ते त्रीण्येतानि सकृत्सकृत्।।

The kings order once, the scholars speak once and the daughter is married off only once. (11)

Certain things require done only once. The repeatitions devalue them. If the king has to repeat his order, it means that the others were not attentive to him which proves that the king is losing respect of others and his authority. That at once weakens his position. Similarly if the scholar has to repeat, it will mean either he was not speaking solemnly or others were not impressed by his wisdom. And in our country a girl is married to a man once in life only. In old times, is was more so. Remarriage of a girl was just unthinkable and was considered a shameful act. Even widows were not allowed to remarry. The society would not accept it. Now attitudes are changing. There are divorces and remarriages.

एकाकिना तपो द्वाभ्यां पठनं गायनं त्रिभिः ।
चतुर्भिर्गमनं क्षेत्रं पञ्चभिर्बहुभिर्रणः ॥

Meditation and the work that requires concentration is done in solitude. Two students together study better. Three singers practising together makes more sense. Four make a better team for undertaking a voyage. Farming takes about five workers to do the job properly. And a lot of persons are required to make an army. (12)

It is a numbers game, Chanakya thinks. Some jobs like meditation are done alone. Two studying together can exchange notes, consult and debate to help each other on. It requires three to sing in chorus for harmony. In voyages, to keep going, telling stories and own experiences to others works fine. Four is no less or too many to give a feeling if security and comeraderie. It takes at least five to work manually in the fields. And of course many soldiers are needed to form an army to fight a war.

सा भार्या या शुचिर्दक्षा सा भार्या या पतिव्रता।
सा भार्या या पतिप्रीता सा भार्या सत्यवादिनी।।

A good wife is one who is pious, expert in household chores, true and faithful to her husband and who never speaks a lie to him. (13)

Picture of a real model wife every husband would dream of. But practically it would be very difficult to find such a woman except in Hindi or Tamil movies. Then, women were also expected to consider their husbands as their gods in old orthodox society. The society expected too much from women.

अपुत्रस्य गृहं शून्यं दिशः शून्यास्तबान्धवाः।
मूर्खस्य हृदयं शून्यं सर्वशून्या दरिद्रता।।

A family without son is barren, a man without kith and kin is an orphan, a stupid person has no feelings and a poor person is barren, orphan and feelingless. (14)

Chanakya feels that the most unfortunate and tragic is one who is poverty stricken. Others has some pain and some sorrow due to various reasons, shortcomings and misfortunes. But a poor person himself is a mass of pain and sorrow. It is most tragic fate. He has nothing and no hope for getting anything. He is abandoned by all. No one comes to his rescue because none likes to spare any time for him even to console. He is so much insulted and humiliated that all his feelings died long ago. Woe that is a poor fellow.

अनभ्यासे विषं शास्त्रमजीर्णे भोजनं विषम्।
दरिद्रस्य विषं गोष्ठी वृद्धस्य तरुणी विषम्।।

Learning without exercise is poison, a meal without appetite is poison, living in society of a poor man is poison and for an old husband, a young wife is poison. (15)

Learning or knowledge is meant to be exercised or put to practical use. Unutilised skill or knowledge degenerates into an evil idea, nothing short of poison. Undigested food turns into acid poison. In society, the poor is always treated to the poison of abuses and insults. An old man with young wife flops around in the pool of the poison of self-pity and impotent rage.

तजेद्धर्मं दयाहीनं विद्याहीनं गुरुं त्यजेत्।
त्यजेत्क्रोधमुखीं भार्यां निःस्नेहान् बान्धवांस्त्यजेत्॥

A man must quit a religion that does not preach love and kindness. Similarly one should leave a teacher who has no knowledge to impart, a woman who has a short temper and relatives who have no love to give. (16)

Love and compassion is the very foundation of every religion, the very essense of it. Any faith not teaching those values is anything but a religion. A woman with short temper would make the domestic life a virtual hell. A man without such wife will be better off. The relatives without love or brotherly feelings are of no use. They won't be around in the hour of need. So, why keep them around when there is no need?

अध्वा जरा मनुष्याणां वाजिनां बन्धनं जरा।
अमैथुनं जरा स्त्रीणां वस्त्राणामातपो जरा॥

A person who is mostly on the travel, gets old in no time. Horses who stand tethered all the time, get old in no time. Woman who are not made love to, get old in no time. Clothes that are kept in the sun most of the time, get faded in no time. (17)

Why Chanakya feels that the travelling makes one age quickly? The reason is simple. In bygone era, proper roads were not there, there were little means of travel and no roadside eateries or motels. People mostly travelled on foot. During day times, the sun was merciless. So, during those days of Chanakya, travel was a tiresome task. It meant pounding the rough tracks under blazing sun on the diet of roasted grams or *sattu*. It was energy sapping. The travellers aged fast.

Without exercise the horses are bound to age or become sick. And woman need love to stay young, healthy and in a positive frame of mind.

कः कालः कानि मित्राणि को देशः कौ व्यायाऽऽगमौ।
कश्चाऽहं का च मे शक्तिरिति चिन्त्यं मुहुर्मुहुः।।

A wise person must always keep in mind the following thoughts being pondered over; How is the time treating me? How many true friends I have made? How is the place I live at? How much do I earn and how do I spend? Who am I and what I am capable of? (18)

Chanakya thinks that one must always assess oneself and analyse all the situations and conditions around him. It will help one take corrective measures in time or plan new agenda for himself to fill the gaps or voids. The constant self-assessment is advised.

जनिता चोपनेता च यस्तु विद्यां प्रयच्छति।
अन्नदाता भयत्राता पञ्चैते पितरः स्मृताः।।

The biological sire, the priest who performs new born's birth rights, the teacher who imparts education, the food provider and protector; the above five are one's fathers. (19)

The above five should be paid respects reserved for the father figure. Here, the sire, the providers and the protector should be one person i.e. one's biological father. Because he earns the bread and provides basic protection as well.

राजपत्नी गुरो: पत्नी मित्रपत्नी तथैव च।
पत्नीमाता स्वमाता च पञ्चैता मातर: स्मृता:।।

The wife of the king, the wife of the teacher, the wife of the friend, the mother of the wife and the biological mother; these five are one's mother figures. (20)

In feudal India the king's wife, fief's wife or zamindar's wife was hailed as *'Rajmata'* by the common folk. Thus, people traditionally accepted the ruler's wife as their *'Royal Mother'*. But a modern person would be reluctant to treat his friend's wife as his mother. The first of all, the friend's wife won't like it and may consider it a slight because it would be like treating her as an old woman. The mindset was different in Chanakya's time.

अग्निर्देवो द्विजातीनां मुनीनां हृदि दैवतम्।
प्रतिमा स्वल्पबुद्धीनां सर्वत्र समदर्शिन:।।

The fire is god of two castes. God of the sages lives in their hearts. God of fools and slow brains lives in idols. But those who have unprejudiced vision, they see God everywhere and in everything. (21)

Here Chanakya unwittingly betrays the fact that he personally thought very little of the practice of idol worship. He had no faith in idols. Infact he is calling idol worshippers as fools and slow brains.

The fire being go of two castes is a mythological belief. The sages used to live in forests to do penance and meditation. They rarely visited any temples. So, there god had to live with them in their hearts.

The Summary of the Chapter

A man's course of life is predetermined at the very time of conception by fate. But the fate is no free distribution agency. The man has to earn what is granted in fate. He must learn, groom, practice, train, work hard and go through the usual grind to realise his fate. Otherwise nothing comes free. Besides working to qualify for the grants of the fate one has to do additional noble deeds, charity and other good things to stay on the credit side.

Chanakya has again extolled the virtues of the education as unseasonal fruit bearer and as protector in the foreign lands. It is a virtual secret treasure chest.

He has compared a bad and foolish son with a life long river of sorrow. A good son, loving wife and peaceful home is heaven for a hard working layman where he can take refuge from the cruel outside world in which he toils all day long.

If a king has to repeat his orders it means he is losing command. A scholar repeating his words is losing respect of others.

No woe is greater than poverty. A poor man's life is devoid of joy, self-respect, honour, hope and love.

Knowledge or learning is to make use of it. Unutilised skill or knowledge rots to become poison to generate evil ideas. If one does not use one's knowledge then devil will hire it.

Woe is an old man who has a young wife. Self-pity and impotent rage roast him. For him the young wife proves a poison.

A religion which does not teach love and compassion is not worth subscribing to. A sweet talking and loving wife is a treasurable thing. So are relatives who have love for you.

A man must always be self-assessing himself by analysing

his current position, the worth of the friends he has made, the situations and conditions around him, about his financial standing, his own worth physically and spiritually and his own capacity to meet challenges of future or to undertake new ventures.

Chanakya has no good word about the practice of idol worship. He terms it as the exercise of fools and slow brains. He prefers to believe in the omnipresence of God.

❑❑

CHAPTER FIVE

Infatuation is the most sickening desease. Greed is the worst enemy. Anger is the worst fire. Knowledge is the most comforting possession.

गुरुरग्निर्द्विजातीनां वर्णानां ब्राह्मणो गुरुः ।
पतिरेव गुरुः स्त्रीणां सर्वस्याऽभ्यागतो गुरुः ।।

The fire is diety of all the upper castes. Brahmin is the guru of all the castes. Husband is the guru of the wife. And a guest is the guru of all of them who deserves everyone's respectful hospitality. (1)

Thus a guest is most revered figure in our society. He is considered the physical form of God. The entire host family is expected to be humble, courteous and respectful to a guest who has kindly graced the house of the host. It does not apply only to the invited guest but an unexpected guest or a shelter seeker who must be accorded the same treatment. It has become part of our culture. In this respect we have been so generous that we extended this treatment to all refugees and even invaders of our country. They comfortably settled down to make this land their own home to make this country as it is today, a mixture of all kinds of people, races and religions.

यथा चतुर्भिः कनकं परीक्ष्यते निघर्षणच्छेदनतापताडनैः ।
तथा चतुर्भिः पुरुष परीक्ष्यते त्यागेन शीलेन गुणेन कर्मणा ।।

The purity of gold is tested by; rubbing, cutting, heating and pounding. Similarly a man's quality can be tested by his gentlemanliness, manners, dealings and character. (2)

The manners immediately shows the man's growing. The rest of the qualities surface in talking, dealing and associating gradually.

तावद् भयेषु भेतव्यं यावद्भयमनागतम् ।
आगतं तु भयं दृष्ट्वा प्रहर्तव्यमशङ्कया ।।

Problems come to everyone. The wise ones rightly are afraid of crisis and troubles when they appear on the horizon. But when they arrive one should get up and boldly face them. (3)

Troubles should be feared of only till they do not show up right in front of one. That is time when efforts should be made to avert their arrival. But if they come, it is no time for fearing. It is time to fight back fiercely instead of being afraid.

एकोदरसमुद्भूता एक नक्षत्रजातकाः ।
न भवन्ति समाः शीले यथा बदरिकण्टकाः ।।

Children born out of the same womb and under the same stars are not a like in qualities and nature. Ber tree's fruits and thorns are not alike in shape, size and taste. (4)

All people are different in nature, attitudes and aptitudes inspite of being born in similar conditions. Everyone has different thumb print. Diversity is the law of nature. No two things are exactly alike. Even twins are different in hundreds of ways.

निःस्पृहो नाऽधिकारी स्यान्नाकामी मण्डनप्रियः ।
नाऽविदग्धः प्रियं ब्रूयात् स्फुटवक्ता न वञ्चकः ।।

All the administrators are corrupt in one way or other.
A person who likes to preen is surely romantic. A person
who is not clever can not be polite talker. A frank person
can not be deceitful. (5)

Administrators are corrupt at least for the desire of
promotion. One who cares for his looks and keeps prettying
himself has got to be a philanderer. Polite talking needs
cleverness cultivated through education. A frank person
can't be a cheat because cheating needs secretiveness and
double talk.

मूर्खाणां पण्डिता द्वेष्या अधनानां महाधनाः ।
वाराऽङ्गनाः कुलस्त्रीणां सुभगानां च दुर्भगाः ।।

Fools are jealous of learned people, poor are jealous
of rich ones, prostitutes hate pious women and widows envy
women with living husbands. (6)

One who lacks somethings is enemy of the one who has
got that something. It is a natural situation. There's a
psychological reason. When a pigmy sees a tall man, he at
once realises his own shortcoming and the pigmy starts
hating the tall man. If the pigmy were never to see a tall man,
he would not hate tallness. So, this jealousy is visual and
situational comparative reaction.

आलस्योपहता विद्या परहस्तगताः स्त्रियः ।
अल्पबीजं हतं क्षेत्रं हतं सैन्यमनायकम् ।।

The idling destroys the learning, the woman gone to
other man gets destroyed, little seeding ruins the harvest
and the death of the commander finishes his army. (7)

Learning is the only kind of treasure that multiplies

when it is given around to others. When not done so, it starts shrinking and dies out. It requires constant updating and revising. The exercise keeps it alive.

A commander leads his army. He is the real force that keeps the soldiers together working like a machine. His commands do it. When he is dead, the army becomes aimless for want of directions. As a result the whole army disintegrates as there is no time for new commander to take over and get set up.

अभ्यासाद्धार्यते विद्या कुलं शीलेन धार्यते ।
गुणेन ज्ञायते त्वार्यः कोपो नेत्रेण गम्यते ।।

Education is gained through regular exercises. A family's class manifests through its good credentials. A great man is recognised by his noble qualities. A man's eyes display his anger. (8)

Regular exercise is needed for learning process. It is the most important part of the education. The real aim of the education is the development of the brain. And that is possible only through exercises. To build up a muscular body one has to do regular physical exercises. Similar is the case with the brain.

The most visible signal of anger is flashed through one's eyes. The eyebrows arch to hood the eyes for more effect. The face darkens to provide better contrast.

वित्तेन रक्ष्यते धर्मो विद्या योगेन रक्ष्यते ।
मृदुना रक्ष्यते भूपः सत्स्त्रिया रक्ष्यते गृहम् ।।

The money protects the religion. The learning can be protected through practice. The politeness protects the king. The pious women protect the home. (9)

It takes money to be religious. Performing rites cost

money. Giving charity and doing good deeds also need proper and liberal financing. Going on pilgrimages requires budget. Most of the festivals are related to religion. That spending also is basically for religion.

The polite words save the ruler. A king who meets his subjects and talks to them in polite words becomes popular. He endears himself to the masses. All it takes is a few polite words and sympathy. The position of such king becomes very strong. As long as people are with him the chieftans dare not hatch any plot against the king. The minister too remain in control. Such king, even if defeated in a war can seek refuge anywhere in his kingdom to rearise. The people will be too glad to hide and help him.

अन्यथा वेदपाण्डित्यं शास्त्रमाचारमन्यथा।
अन्यथा कुवचः शान्तं लोकाः क्लिश्यन्ति चान्यथा।।

Curse be on the people who; talk ill of the learning of a scholarly one, say that rituals stated in the scriptures are useless and call a serene person a hypocrat and imposter. They will suffer. (10)

Some persons make fun of the scholarly person and ridicule his learning. For them everything written in ancient scriptures is rubbish. And one who believes in them is fool. A learned person is serene and no big mouth. His serenity is taken for cowardice or surrender. Such talk does not harm the scholar in anyway. But the people who talk like that themselves suffer.

दारिद्र्यनाशनं दानं शीलं दुर्गतिनाशनम्।
अज्ञाननाशिनी प्रज्ञा भावना भयनाशिनी।।

The charity destroys poverty. Good behaviour keeps troubles away. The wisdom washes away ignorance and stupidity. Devotion to God expells fear. (11)

In our culture, charity has been excessively praised. One of the reasons is that during middle ages there were large number of people who lived on charity namely Brahmins, Sadhus, Fakirs, holymen, monks, beggars and poor. The economy benefitted a few people. They had to be induced to be charitable for the benefit of the alms seekers. So, it was said that charity did not eat away the rich man's wealth to assure him. The blessings it earned, the goodwill it generated and the fame it brought, was in fact impressive which pleased the charity giver. In some way it benefitted the business of the donor also which compensated the spending on the charity.

The rest of the advices is easy to follow and do not need any elaboration.

नाऽस्ति कामसमो व्याधिर्नाऽस्ति मोहसमो रिपुः।
नाऽस्ति कोपसमो वह्निर्नाऽस्ति ज्ञानात् परं सुखम्।।

Infatuation is the most sickening desease. Greed is the biggest enemy. Anger is the worst fire. And knowledge is the most comforting possession. (12)

Infatuation makes the infatuated person lose his mind. He is beyond any reasoning and listens to no one's advice. His mind is deseased with just one obsession, to get the person or thing he desires. In such state he does something stupid and pays a heavy price.

The greed leads to one's downfall. It never does any good, just like an enemy. And like fire, the anger does a person great harm. It burns away his relationships with others. Acts done in anger haunt one throughout one's life.

Knowledge is the most beneficial of one's assets. The wisdom creates an oasis of peace in one's mind.

जन्ममृत्यू हि यात्येको भुनक्त्येकः शुभाऽशुभम्।
नरकेषु पतत्येक एको याति परां गतिम्।।

A human comes into this world alone. Alone does he get the reward or punishment for good deeds or sins respectively. And alone he departs for heavenly abode. (13)

A man is responsible for his own acts. He can't blame anyone else for whatever befalls him. One negotiates his life himself. Thus, a man must act very carefully knowing fully well that no one will share his burden. If he does noble deeds he will earn all the rewards. No one will take away anything. Similarly, no one else can borrow your pain, this life is a one man show.

तृणं ब्रह्मविदः स्वर्गस्तृणं शूरस्य जीवितम्।
जिताऽशस्य तृणं नारी निःस्पृहस्य तृणं जगत्।।

One who knows the ultimate truth, the heaven is of little significance. For a warrior, life is nothing. For an ascetic, a woman means little. And for one who has conquered desires, the whole world is absolute nothing. (14)

The ultimate truth is that the final aim of a soul is to unite with God. Attain *moksha* (Nirvana). The heaven is insignificant distraction. This world holds no attraction for a person who has given up all desires. He is not like ordinary one who is trapped in desires. He does not try to chase mirages or catch shadows. He is the truly liberated one.

विद्या मित्रं प्रवासेषु भार्या मित्रं गृहेषु च।
व्याधितस्यौषधं मित्रं धर्मो मित्रं मृतस्य च।।

Skill is a man's friend in a foreign land. A good natured wife is the man's best friend. Medicine is a sick man's friend. And charitable deeds are one's only friend after death. (15)

In this couplet Chanakya tells us about friends in need who are friends indeed. Education in some skill or field comes good in a foreign land. It helps find employment quickly. The life partener is a man's best friend, no doubt provided she is not quarrelsome. After death only the goodness of the good deeds done by the deceased goes as credit with the soul. The credit is supposed to open the doors of the heaven. The Hindu belief is that this credit is carried forward to the next life as advantage points to be adjusted in grants of fate.

वृथा वृष्टिः समुद्रेषु वृथा तृप्तेषु भोजनम् ।
वृथा दानं धनाढ्येषु वृथा दीपो दिवाऽपि च ।।

The rain over ocean, feeding a person who is already fed, giving donations to rich and lighting up lamp in broad daylight; these are meaningless exercises. (16)

No elaboration required—The couplet is so clear in itself that commenting on it would be another meaningless exercise.

नास्ति मेघसमं तोयं नास्ति चात्मसमं बलम् ।
नास्ति चक्षुःसमं तेजो नास्ति धान्यसमं प्रियम् ।।

The clouds carry the purest water, will-power is the mightiest power, vision of eyes is the brightest light and the food is the most satisfying thing. (17)

The clouds have the distilled water in vapour form. Will-power can make the impossible happen. The eyesight makes the light meaningful. And naturally food is the basic drive of all creatures. It creates the most enjoyable sensory pleasures. Food is so elementary that when one gets suddenly rich the first thing one wants to do is to eat what he always wanted to. And in a country which has suffered centuries of poverty and food shortages it gains more significance. In Chanakya's time the situation was grim. Most of the people never had enough to eat.

अधना धनमिच्छन्ति वाचं चैव चतुष्पदाः।
मानवाः स्वर्गमिच्छन्ति मोक्षमिच्छन्ति देवताः।।

A poor man desires for money. The animals desire power of speech, humans desire for heaven and angels desire for Nirvana. (18)

In this universe every one wants something. No one is satisfied. Even angels are no exception. A true contentment eludes all.

सत्येन धार्यते पृथिवी सत्येन तपते रविः।
सत्येन वाति वायुश्च सर्वं सत्ये प्रतिष्ठितम्।।

The truth keeps the earth in its place, the truth makes the sun shine, the truth blows the air and thus the truth is the prime force. (19)

God is nothing but ultimate truth. The space is truth. The matter in space is solid form of the truth. The truth is the soul and matter of this universe. But truth defies any exact definition. No religion has ever been able to explain it. All the forces that influence the cosmos and run through it are also forms of truth. The truth about the truth is the last mystery that man will have to solve.

चला लक्ष्मीश्चलाः प्राणाश्चलं जीवित-यौवनम्।
चलाचले च संसारे धर्म एको हि निश्चलः।।

In this world nothing lasts forever. The money comes and then goes. The life goes. The soul goes. The youth goes. The only thing that stays firm is the faith. (20)

The only thing that is permanent is this world is the faith. There are different faiths. They all represent a desire to meet God. All faiths are different paths supposed to lead us to our Creator. This undying wish to reach God will survive everything. It is the only permanent thing.

नराणां नापितो धूर्तः पक्षिणां चैव वायसः।
चतुष्पदां शृगालस्तु स्त्रीणां धूर्ता च मालिनी।।

Among men barber is the cleverest and the trickiest guy. Among birds crow and among animals jackal is the most cunning. And among women flower seller is the most naughty. (21)

In our society the barber is the professional match-maker. He has to be clever because his task is tricky. He must act as go between and bring the families together to help strike the marital deal. And flowerseller used to go to every home, in old times, to deliver daily flowers for ladies. On the side, she acted as messenger between families and lovers as she had access to every home. In due course she learned to play naughty tricks and games fuelling quarrels, breaking up affairs and arranging new alignments. And she was the keeper of every one's secrets.

The Summary of the Chapter

In this chapter Chanakya has revealed the great respect that our society accords to a guest. In him the host sees God.

He advises us to deal with problems and troubles boldly giving up all fear.

It is essential to keep the education and learning protected. Neglect and idling can erode knowledge. The process of learning is best served through regular exercises. The effort of learning new things must be always continued.

The money given in charity is not a debit. It brings back manifold credit in the form of goodwill and fame which earns more business. It also gets goodness to open the doors of the heaven for the donor.

He has listed infatuation, greed and anger as vices one

should avoid. Man has to bear the burdens of his misdeeds alone because life is a one man show. Only good deeds help when the end comes.

No one is satisfied in this world. Everyone wants something. Hence, best solution is to be content and wish for no more.

There is also mention of faith as the biggest stabilising factor in this shaky world. The truth is soul, matter and force of this cosmos. God is nothing but ultimate truth which every faith is trying to reach.

❑❑

CHAPTER SIX

You can win over; a greedy by offer of money, a proud person by cowering before him, a fool by agreeing with him and a scholar by speaking the truth.

श्रुत्वा धर्मं विजानाति श्रुत्वा त्यजति दुर्मतिम् ।
श्रुत्वा ज्ञानमवाप्नोति श्रुत्वा मोक्षमवाप्नुयात् ।।

By hearing the scriptures recited one learns the secrets of the religion. By listening to the talk of a scholar, an evil person gets rid of evil thoughts. And the advice of spiritual guru opens the doors of heaven and way to Nirvana beyond. (1)

It is the spiritual guru listening to whom benefits one most. An able spiritual guru can guide one's soul to its ultimate aim of achieving the state of *Nirvana*, the union with God.

पक्षिणां काकश्चाण्डालः पशूनां चैव कुक्कुरः ।
मुनीनां कोपी चाण्डालः सर्वेषां चैव निन्दकः ।।

Among birds the crow is the most evil, among animals

dog, among sages the short tempered one and among common folk the back-biter is the worst evil. (2)

The crow is worst because it lives on human filth. The dog does not find favour with Chanakya, perhaps because the dog has dislike for Brahmins. In western countries the dogs hate postmen. May be, when Brahmins come to the house of their clients barking dogs are the first ones to greet them. And most of the Brahmins carry lathis which arouses hostile reaction in the dogs. The short tempered Munis are notorious for giving curses. Of course, back-biter is the worst human. They harm others for no reason and create misunderstandings. They enjoy doing so because they are evil through and through.

भस्मना शुध्यते कांस्यं ताम्रमम्लेन शुध्यति।
रजसा शुध्यते नारी नदी वेगेन शुध्यति।।

The brass pot can be cleaned with ash, copper gets cleaned with citric acids, monthly period purifies women and the river water becomes potable after flowing through rapids. (3)

There are different cleansing systems for different items. The nature has its own methods to clean things and bodies periodically. Similary humans must clean their items from time to time to create healthy environment.

भ्रमन् सम्पूज्यते राजा भ्रमन् सम्पूज्यते द्विजः।
भ्रमन् सम्पूज्यते योगी स्त्री भ्रमन्ती विनश्यति।।

A king who tours the countryside to know the state of the people is adored by masses. A preacher who lectures in foreign lands is respected. A yogi who undertakes travels far and wide is very appreciated. But a woman who takes to road gets desecrated. (4)

The first three benefit by undertaking travels. But it does no good to a woman because the family and the society has not trained her to deal with the world outside which is hostile to a single woman. A woman outside quickly attracts attention of others, especially of the bad elements. A lonely woman on her own gives them evil ideas. She can't defend herself physically. There are others who lay traps for such targets. A woman is too soft and does not know the ways of the world. She can be easily tricked or led astray. She has no chance of surviving in such a world except surrendering to the wishes of the rogue elements or tricksters. Once in a trap her entire future is ruined. She has no escape and all the roads of return are closed to her.

तादृशी जायते बुद्धिर्व्यवसायोऽपि तादृशः ।
सहायास्तादृशा एव यादृशी भवितव्यता ।।

One who has money, he has lot of friends and lines of relatives. He is hailed as a real man. He is also considered full of wisdom. (5)

Money is the real power. It has always been so. It spells success. Everything he does is okay. The friends and relatives dance around the man who has money. The money makes him the women's fovourite man, the symbol of manhood. He is the wise one also. Chanakya accepts the fact that the money buys almost everything.

कालः पचति भूतानि कालः संहरते प्रजाः ।
कालः सुप्तेषु जागर्ति कालो हि दुरतिक्रमः ।।

The time consumes all creatures. It kills every one. It is awake while people sleep. No one can escape from its consuming power. (6)

The time is the mightiest of all. It is a death warrant

against all creatures and everything. As soon as a child is born it begins count-down to serve the warrant at zero count. It sees everyone but no one has ever seen it. It is timing all of us on its hit-list.

न पश्यति च जन्मान्धः कामान्धो नैव पश्यति।
न पश्यति मदोन्मत्तो ह्यर्थी दोषान् न पश्यति।।

A born blind can't see, so does a man blinded with passion of love. A drunkard can't see what is good or what is bad. And a selfish man is also blind to the evil of his actions done to achieve the selfish goal. (7)

A lusting man, a drunkard and a selfish person are no better than a blind man. They are blind to the reality, to the reason and to the fairness of actions. Even people with eyes can be blind in many ways.

स्वयं कर्म करोत्यात्मा स्वयं तत्फलमश्नुते।
स्वयं भ्रमति संसारे स्वयं तस्माद्विमुच्यते।।

A person commits acts and faces the consequences himself. He takes birth in many life forms and eventually dares to break free from all the life cycles and joins his Creator. (8)

It is Hindu philosophy. A soul is supposed to be trapped in endless life and death circles. It goes on until in some life he realises his purpose of taking births. Then he performs the required deeds to get liberated and his soul attains *moksha*, the union with God.

राजा राष्ट्रकृतं भुंक्ते राज्ञः पापं पुरोहितः।
भर्ता च स्त्रीकृतं पापं शिष्यपापं गुरुस्तथा।।

A king pays for the sins of his people, the royal priest pays for the sins of the king and the husband pays for the sins of his wife. Similarly a teacher pays for the sins of his pupil. (9)

A king is morally responsible for all works, actions, deeds and misdeeds of the people of his kingdom. Being a moral advisor, the royal priest is responsible for king's doings. If the king goes wrong the priest must try to correct him by giving suitable advice. A man is answerable for his wife's actions or behaviour. It is the duty of a teacher to keep his charge straight. He should pay for the failings of his pupil.

ऋणकर्ता पिता शत्रुः माता च व्यभिचारिणी ।
भार्या रूपवती शत्रुः पुत्रः शत्रुरपण्डितः ।।

A father who leaves behind unpaid debts is the enemy of his children. A mother with loose character is a shame for her children. A beautiful wife is also enemy of her husband. And a foolish son is enemy of his parents. (10)

A father who dies leaving debts behind ruins his children. The children never get chance to start the life properly because paying back the debts becomes their first task. The burden stops their growth as well. Having a mother of loose character makes the life of her children shameful. They are never treated with honour and respect. The lives of such children are spent in hiding their faces. For a husband a beautiful wife is a great handicap. Everyone eyes her with evil intentions. The husband spends his time worrying for her instead of concentrating on his work. He is in physical danger too. Remember how prince Jahangir got the husband of Noorjahan killed when the prince wanted her for himself?

लुब्धमर्थेन गृह्णीयात् स्तब्धमञ्जलिकर्मणा ।
मूर्खं छन्दोऽनुवृत्तेन यथार्थत्वेन पण्डितम् ।।

The following can be won over; a greedy by offer of money, a proud person by cowering before him, a fool by agreeing with him and a scholar by speaking the truth. (11)

A greedy can be bought. If you cower and act like a beggar before a vain person his ego gets satisfied and he would like to reward you by granting your wish. If you agree with a fool, he is impressed and pleased with you because you make him feel a wise person. He will do anything you say in return. It is a rare honour for him. A scholar values truthfulness. It is because a scholar is mostly surrounded by loud mouthed people, flatterers and politicians who never speak truth. He yearns to hear some true and frank talk.

वरं न राज्यं न कुराजराज्यं वरं न मित्रं न कुमित्रमित्रम् ।
वरं न शिष्यो न कुशिष्यशिष्यो वरं न दारा न कुदारदाराः ।।

It is better to have no state instead of having a bad state. Better to have no friends instead of having evil friends. Better to have no pupil instead of having bad pupil. Better to have no wife instead of being the husband of a bad wife. (12)

It would be better to give no comment instead of giving one where it is not needed.

कुराजराज्येन कुतः प्रजासुखं कुमित्रमित्रेण कुतोऽस्ति निर्वृतिः ।
कुदारदारैश्च कुतो गृहे रतिः कुशिष्यमध्यापयतः कुतो यशः ।।

There is no happiness in the kingdom of an evil king. There comes no good from a deceitful friend. There is no joy or peace in the home where lives an evil wife. There is no glory for a teacher in teaching a bad pupil. (13)

Bad people bring no good results. It will be a rank foolishness if one planted a thorny Ber tree and hoped to reap the harvest of sweet mangoes.

सिंहादेकं बकादेकं शिक्षेच्चत्वारि कुक्कुटात् ।
वायसात्पञ्च शिक्षेच्च षट् शुनस्त्रीणि गर्दभात् ।।

Every creature has some special quality about it which can serve as example or lesson for humans to learn things. The lion and crane teach us one lesson each. A cock has four, a crow five, a dog six and a donkey has three lessons to impart to us. They are as following—(14)

प्रभूतं कार्यमल्पं वा यन्नरः कर्तुमिच्छति।
सर्वारम्भेण तत्कार्यं सिंहादेकं प्रचक्षते।।

Whatever the project a person has to execute, the lion teaches us to begin it with full thrust of your power and not to relax till the task is completed. (15)

A lion plans the attack and then springs on its target with full force and does not relax its holds till the prey dies.

इन्द्रियाणि च संयम्य बकवत् पण्डितो नरः।
देशकालबलं ज्ञात्वा सर्वकार्याणि साधयेत्।।

A clever man must concentrate his attention on his goal just like a crane. When it spots a fish it stands immobile, eyes fixed on the target. (16)

Upon sighting a target fish the crane freezes its body. The eyes are fixed on the fish. Its mind calculates the distance, direction, and force required. At right time it strikes at right place with right force.

It treaches importance of concentration.

प्रत्युत्थानं च युद्धं च संविभागं च बन्धुषु।
स्वयमाक्रम्य भुक्तं च शिक्षेच्चत्वारि कुक्कुटात्।।

The cock imparts four lessons; rising early, being ever ready to defend or attack, giving due shares to others and grabbing own share of food. (17)

A cock gives a wake-up call to every one every morning. It is always ready to defend its roost by attacking anyone who dares to intrude into his territory. It generously offers feed to hens and the brood. And it pecks its own food aggressively.

गूढमैथुनचरित्वं च काले काले च संग्रहम् ।
अप्रमत्तमविश्वासं पञ्च शिक्षेच्च वायसात् ।।

The crow teaches to make love in privacy, to be obstinate, to collect things for later use, to be ever alert and to not to trust anyone fully. These five lessons the crow teaches. (18)

The crow is obstinate. It does not get scared away easily. It is always testing the things it finds and collects some desirable items for close analysis. It is always alert and watchful. It likes no surprises. The crow never really trusts anyone, the secret of its survival in human colonies.

बह्वाशी स्वल्पसन्तुष्टः सुनिद्रो लघुचेतनः ।
स्वामिभक्तश्च शूरश्च षडेते श्वानतो गुणाः ।।

When dog gets food, it overeats. If it does not get to eat anything, it is not worried. It just goes to sleep contentedly. But even a slight noise wakes it up. The dog is a very loyal pet and never is shy of fighting ferociously. Learn these six lessons from a dog. (19)

The dog does not overeat to get sick. It has the capacity to hold food. Some extra in stomach gives it enough confidence to not to worry about the next meal. While it sleeps, its ears stay awake to send warning signal to brain, functioning like sound-activated electronic gadget. And its loyalty is a legend and the fighting spirit is well known.

सुश्रान्तोऽपि वहेद् भारं शीतोष्णं न च पश्यति ।
सन्तुष्टश्चरते नित्यं त्रीणि शिक्षेच्च गर्दभात् ।।

The donkey teaches us three things; to work tirelessly for the master, stoicity and contendedness. (20)

The donkey never refuses any work. It just goes on and on. The heat or cold don't make any impression on it. It's fine for it always. And it never complains.

य एतान् विंशतिगुणानाचरिष्यति मानवः।
कार्याऽवस्थासु सर्वासु अजेयः स भविष्यति।।

A person who imbibes these twenty qualities and makes them part of his character, he is successful in all endeavours in all conditions. The failure is not his lot. He is a winner all the way.

The Summary of the Chapter

The most striking thing in this chapter is the twenty lessons we can learn from various creatures to emerge a winner in all our endeavours. The lessons are as under—

The Lion : It stalks the prey, pounces on it with full force, grabs it and does not relax its hold till the job of killing is executed.

Similarly a man must plan, launch the project with full force and keep up the pressure until the project is not completed.

The Crane : It spots fish, immobilises its entire body, calculates all the aspects of the attack during the frozen period; the time, place, distance, angle, force required, speed etc. Then it attacks. In a flash the fish is taken.

Similarly, a man must concentrate on his project and calculate all the requirements minutely before beginning it.

The Donkey : Learn three things from donkey; work tirelessly be stoic and don't complain. You will become favourite worker of your employer. If you are your own master, then, you will achieve greater things.

The Cock : The cock teaches us four things; getting up early in the morning. Defending your interests zealously like the cock defends its roost. Giving others their due share. Claiming your share rightfully without letting anyone steal it.

The Crow : Imbibe five qualities or characteristics a crow displays; Make love in privacy. Don't make it a *tamasha*. Walk quietly. Examine the things you come across and collect the desirables. Be ever vigilant like a crow. Don't let others scare you away. And do not put your faith totally in any one else.

The Dog : It has six things to teach us: Eat well, Don't worry if the next food is delayed. Sleep well. But be careful and wake up at the slightest disturbance like a dog does. Be loyal to your master or to your friends or whoever is important to you. Be brave and fight if needed.

❏❏

CHAPTER SEVEN

*Do not be too simple and too straight.
Go to the jungle to see how the smooth
and straight trees have been cut down
mercilessly but the crooked ones stand
unharmed.*

अर्थनाशं मनस्तापं गृहे दुश्चरितानि च।
वञ्चनं चाऽपमानं च मतिमान्न प्रकाशयेत्।।

A wise person must not reveal on others; the loss of money, the deep wound of heart, scandal of the family, the incidents of getting cheated or insulted. (1)

The information on the loss of money can harm your stature and financial standing in the society. And the other matters mentioned like pain of heart, scandal, cheating and insult also may work the same way. The people are more interested in rubbing salt in wounds rather than applying balm. All the above tips are just the material that back biters, gossip mongers and rumour spreaders need to run you down. They can do irreparable damage. You will lose the respect of others and become a laughing stock. It also reveals how naive, simple and vulnerable you can be. This will give ideas

to others to play the same kind of tricks on you. Don't show
your soft belly to others and expose your weak points.

धन-धान्यप्रयोगेषु   विद्यासंग्रहणेषु   च ।
आहारे व्यवहारे च त्यक्तलज्जः सुखी भवेत् ।।

*A person who is shameless (bold) in the matters of;
dealings in money or trade, learning some art or skill,
eating and behaviour, is a happy one. (2)*

In dealing a man must show bold, shameless approach
to make the terms clear leaving no room for any
misunderstanding. Then the deal will go through smoothly
causing no problems and giving no chance to the other party
to play tricks. Similar boldness is needed while learning
something or at dinner table. The frankness and straight
manner is always beneficial. A hesitant diner remains hungry.
Boldness is infact not a thing of shame. That is why it is said
that a person becomes happy once he learns to say 'No'.
Those who don't know how to say 'no' get trapped in
impossible commitments and end up sad people.

सन्तोषाऽमृत-तृप्तानां यत्सुखं शान्तचेतसाम् ।
न च तद् धनलुब्धानामितश्चेतश्च धावताम् ।।

*A real happy is a man whose mind is at peace and the
heart is content. Running around to amass wealth and
money can't give happiness. (3)*

There is no end to desires and no end to things available.
However rich one might become there is more money outside
which does not belong to him. That fact never lets a rich man
have any peace. The best way is to learn to be content with
whatever one has got.

सन्तोषस्त्रिषु कर्तव्यः स्वदारे भोजने धने ।
त्रिषु चैव न कर्तव्योऽध्ययने तपदानयोः ।।

Be content with what you have already got as wife, food and income. But don't ever be content with your knowledge, self-improvement and charity. (4)

The knowledge, self-improvement and charity have limitless scope. The more one has, the better it is. Hence, one should not be, ever satisfied with what one has got of these things. One must strive for more and more. One can never have enough of these.

The first three items are good to be contented with, namely wife, food and income.

विप्रयोर्विप्रवह्न्योश्च दम्पत्योः स्वामिभृत्ययोः ।
अन्तरेण न गन्तव्यं हलस्य वृषभस्य च ।।

Do not walk through between; two scholars, fire and priest, man and woman, master and his servant and plough-oxen. (5)

Above cited five pairs are such that each pair has some visible or invisible link between them, breaking which is not welcome. Infact, it would be a very objectional and irritating act. The scholars are mostly discussing some matter. If someone comes between them it interrupts their talk making them angry. Fire is in front of the priest only when yagna or *pooja* is being performed. A husband and wife don't tolerate anything causing their separation. Same is the case with a master and his servant. They are infact one unit, the master symbolising its head and the servant its tail. And a plough and the pair of oxen are visibly and physically united.

पादाभ्यां न स्पृशेदग्निं गुरुं ब्राह्मणमेव च।
नैव गां न कुमारीं च न वृद्धं न शिशुं तथा।।

One should never try to touch with one's foot the following; fire, teacher, Brahmin, cow, girl, seniors and a baby. (6)

According to our cultural values, the above seven are considered very respectable in different ways. And touching something with foot is an act of sacrilege, a mark of disrespect which is strongly disapproved and often invites angry protest or rebuke. In case of fire the foot can get burnt as well.

शकटं पञ्चहस्तेन दशहस्तेन वाजिनम्।
हस्ती शतहस्तेन देशत्यागेन दुर्जनम्।।

Keep a distance from a bullock cart by five arm-lengths, a horse by ten arm-lengths, an elephant by thousand arm-lengths. And in case of an evil person get out of the country right away. (7)

Chanakya has in a very illustrative way demonstrated the danger an evil person posses. The arm lengths show the degree of the danger a particular beast posses. An evil person is tens of million times more harmful than the threat of the beastliest of the beasts. A beast can cause only physical harm but an evil person can corrupt one's mind, soul, honour and reputation as well.

हस्ती अंकुशमात्रेण वाजी हस्तेन ताड्यते।
शृङ्गी लगुडहस्तेन खड्गहस्तेन दुर्जनः।।

A goad controls the elephant, a whip controls the horse, a stick controls the cattle but an evil person can be dealt with only a sword. (8)

Here Chanakya is again on the hunt for an evil person. He feels that evil person is beyond any reform. The evil person is incapable of mending his ways. Counseling or reasoning will not work. Such person is fit only for a sword treatment. Cut his head off and finish the evil.

तुष्यन्ति भोजने विप्रा मयूरा घनगर्जिते ।
साधवः परसम्पत्तौ खलः परविपत्तिषु ।।

The sight of food makes a Brahmin happy, the rumble of clouds delights a peacock, the good fortune of others pleases the noble souls and the misfortune of others makes an evil person gleeful. (9)

Nothing good comes out of an evil person. When calamity falls on people and tragedies strike making everyone sad, grief stricken, ruined and tearful, the evil person dances with joy. Such is the perfideious character of an evil soul.

अनुलोमेन बलिनं प्रतिलोमेन दुर्जनम् ।
आत्मतुल्यबलं शत्रुं विनयेन बलेन वा ।।

A mightier enemy can be appeased by humbly obeying his orders, a lesser enemy should be ordered to do as dictated. But in case of a enemy who is equal in power, appeasement or dictation, any of the policy can be adopted as the situation demands. (10)

Chanakya, here, advises the application of diplomacy according to the situation and the status of the enemy involved. Dealing with an equally powerful enemy requires careful evaluation of the positions and situations.

बाहुवीर्यं बलं राज्ञो ब्राह्मणो ब्रह्मविद् बली ।
रूपयौवनमाधुर्यं स्त्रीणां बलमुत्तमम् ।।

Sword is the power of the king. Knowledge is the power of the scholar and beauty and sweetness is the power of the women. (11)

What Chanakya has said here is clear in itself. No elaboration is required.

नाऽत्यन्तं सरलैर्भाव्यं गत्वा पश्य वनस्थलीम् ।
छिद्यन्ते सरलास्तत्र कुब्जास्तिष्ठन्ति पादपाः ।।

Do not be too simple and too straight. Go to the jungle to see how the smooth and the straight trees have been cut down and the crooked ones stand unharmed. (12)

The world is no good for simple and straight people. People often take them for foolish ones and mercilessly exploit them. In this world of crooks, the simple and straight ones stand little chance. Like trees they are cut down and destroyed by exploiters, crooks, crafty and cuning people. They are the losers in the survival game.

यत्रोदकं तत्र वसन्ति हंसाः तथैव शुष्कं परिवर्जयन्ति ।
न हंसतुल्येन नरेण भाव्यं पुनस्त्यजन्ते पुनराश्रयन्ते ।।

The swans live in lakes filled with blue waters. When any lake dries up, the swans of that lake desert it. Men should not change their base too often like swans. (13)

A man can't afford be like swans. Because a man lives a different kind of life. A man makes a lot of investments in the place where he is stationed. It is his base where he has built home, set up his work or business, made friends and aquaintances, built up goodwill and relationships. That is tremendous investment. His entire future and dreams are rooted there. He has memories and emotional attachments with that place. He just can't fly away like a swan. The man must stay back and face the hardships if some calamity has befallen that place. The hard times must be seen through courageously. A man who is footloose makes no progress like a rooling stone that gathers no mass.

उपार्जितानां वित्तानां त्याग एव हि रक्षणम् ।
तडागोदरसंस्थानां परीवाह इवाऽम्भसाम् ।।

Money earned must be spent to keep it in circulation. Put it to good use which is the best protective investment. The water of pond has inflow and outflow systems. That keeps its water clean. (14)

The capital should not be allowed to stagnate and remain as a dead investment. It must be made to work by investing in good projects. That's how it will stay active and will grow for the benefit of all. And it is more safe and alive that way, similarly as the circulation keeps pond water fresh, clean and free of germs.

यस्याऽर्थास्तस्य मित्राणि यस्याऽर्थास्तस्य बान्धवाः ।
यस्याऽर्थाः स पुमांल्लोके यस्याऽर्थाः स च जीवति ।।

In the human world, money is the driving force. One who has money makes friends and relatives. He is treated as the real man and women fawn over him. Money makes him the wise one. And he lives a life of luxury and honour. (15)

Chanakya has frankly admitted the power of money. A man with money has friends and relatives fawning over him. Money whitewashes all the short-comings of a rich man. Because of money he is the epitom of wisdom, success, the most charming, graceous, kind, clever, desirable and capable. In parties he is a sought after figure. Charity seekers throng around him. The TV channels vie to show him. Newspapers and magazines feature him as self-made man and the future of the country.

स्वर्गस्थितानामिह जीवलोके चत्वारि चिह्नानि वसन्ति देहे।
दानप्रसङ्गो मधुरा च वाणी देवाऽर्चनं ब्राह्मणतर्पणं च।।

Those are enjoying heavenly living on earth who show following signs; charitable nature; polite behaviour, faith in God and readiness to serve Brahmin with good food. (16)

The literal translation of the first part of the couplet is; "Those who show the following four signs are considered to be directly descended from heaven"; It looked odd to us because the qualities mentioned are general and ordinary. It is doubtful what exactly Chanakya meant.

अत्यन्तकोपः कटुका च वाणी दरिद्रता च स्वजनेषु वैरम्।
नीचप्रसङ्गः कुलहीनसेवा चिह्नानि देहे नरकस्थितानाम्।।

In Virtual hell are those who are short-tempered, harsh talkers, poor, quarrelsome, friends of evil people and who serve lowly men. (17)

The above mentioned characters are capable of creating hell for themselves. Those who are short-tempered and bad tongued, they will themselves create enemies. In a short period they will find themselves surrounded by enemies. Every one would be roaring to settle scores with them. A poor man rots in the hell of loneliness because no one would like to be near him. A quarrelsome person is the cousin brother of ill-tempered and harsh tongued ones. He will also suffer the same fate. And one who has evil people for friends he is courting disasters. He will be in trouble in little time.

गम्यते यदि मृगेन्द्र-मन्दिरं लभ्यते करिकपोलमौक्तिकम्।
जम्बुकाऽऽलयगते च प्राप्यते वत्स-पुच्छ-खर-चर्म-खण्डनम्।।

If one goes near the den of a lion one might find precious mani-pearl. But near the den of a jackal one would only find tail of a calf or a piece of donkey hide. (18)

We have already explained in a previous chapter that mani-pearl is fabled gem supposed to develop inside the forehead of an elephant of heavenly breed. Here the supposition is that lion could have killed some such elephant and the gem be around there fallen off the skull. The real message is that going to a person of high class can prove profitable in many ways. But going near a lowly person would get one lowly, unhealthy and useless things, not worth even picking up.

शुनः पुच्छमिव व्यर्थं जीवितं विद्यया विना।
न गुह्यगोपने शक्तं न च दंशनिवारणे।।

A dog's tail can't cover its shame. And it is not made for driving away flies or mosquitoes. So is little knowledge of a man. (19)

Here reference is to short tail of a dog which serves no purpose. A man's little or inadequate education has been compared with the short tail because it is as useless as dog's short tail.

वाचः शौचं च मनसः शौचमिन्द्रियनिग्रहः।
सर्वभूते दया शौचं एतच्छौचं पराऽर्थिनाम्।।

A polite talker, pure at heart, self-disciplined and compassionate to all creatures; these are the signs of one who is qualified for Nirvana. (20)

The message is simple enough to need any comments.

पुष्पे गन्धं तिले तैलं काष्ठेऽग्निं पयसि घृतम्।
इक्षौ गुडं तथा देहे पश्याऽऽत्मानं विवेकतः।।

The flowers have fragrance, oilseeds have oil, wood has fire, milk has butter and cane has sugar in it but we can't see these with our eyes. In the similar way a soul exists in the body which is invisible. It is a mystery that only can be understood through faith and logic. (21)

This couplet also needs no elaboration as it very logically worded and put forward.

The Summary of the Chapter

You must be very guarded about your loss of money, pain of the heart, family scandal, incidents of getting tricked or humiliated. Revealing them will put your honour in danger. You financial standing will become suspect in the eyes of the others. And it will give others a handle to ridicule you, make fun of you and give chances to others to exploit your week points. The people will start doubting your wisdom and capability.

You should be frank in your dealings to avoid any misunderstanding. Be bold in dealings, learning some skill and at meals. Or others will take advantage of your timidity and you will short change yourself.

Don't walk through disrupting the pairs of scholars, husband and wife, master and valet etc. It's rude and unwelcome act.

Misfortunes and tragedies of others pleases the heart of an evil person. He is incorrigible. You can't make such person mend his ways. The best way to deal with an evil person is to put him to death by sword. Or put as big as possible a distance between you and such evil soul.

You must not behave like a nomad, shifting place every now and then. A man must make a home base, a permanent station to have roots to lend stability to your life. It will help you build home, set up workshop or business, make friends . and have neighbours and aquaintances, generate goodwill and trust. All this will inspire you to plan for future.

Being too simple and too straight is no good. You must learn the ways of the world. Become a survivor. In forests straight trees are cut down but the crooked ones are not harmed. That's how the world is. The simple people are exploited. Being a little crafty and cunning is essential in the world of crooks to stay alive.

The money should not be allowed to become a dead capital. It must be invested in good projects to make it generate more money.

There are many things which exist but are not visible to the naked eye like the fragrance of the flowers. Similarly a soul exists within a body but no one ever sees it. Only faith and logic can explain its existence.

Always try to stay near good and noble people. You will gain. Stationing near or deviating toward the lowly people will gain you lowly and undesirable objects or qualities only.

❑❑

CHAPTER EIGHT

A great dynasty is no great if it is bereft of educated members. If a person of low birth gains learning and wisdom, he would be honourable for nobles even.

अधमा धनमिच्छन्ति धनं मानं च मध्यमाः।
उत्तमा मानमिच्छन्ति मानो हि महतां धनम्।।

In this world, those who desire only wealth are lowly people of lowest level. Those who desire wealth and respect are people of middle level. The persons of highest level only desire honour and respect. (1)

The people of highest level work only for honour and respect. And glory comes in the bargain. These can be attained through educationing and learning. One has to excel in certain field and become an achiever. In ancient times there were very limited choices available. Today, there are hundreds of fields where one can make a mark and earn recognition.

इक्षुरापः पयो मूलं ताम्बूलं फलमौषधम्।
भक्षयित्वाऽपि कर्तव्याः स्नानदानाऽऽदिकाः क्रियाः।।

Taking bath and religious acts can be performed even after taking cane, water, milk, fruits, paan and medicines. (2)

There is a traditional belief that eats and drinks should be taken only after bath and meditation or prayer. Nothing before that. Here Chanakya is advising otherwise in special circumstances like illness.

दीपो भक्षयते ध्वान्तं कज्जलं च प्रसूयते।
यदन्नं भक्षयेन्नित्यं जायते तादृशी प्रजा।।

The oil lamp eats away darkness and produces soot. Similarly a person breeds offspring according to the kind of food he eats. (3)

Here Chanakys is not talking of the physical nature of the food. It is the spiritual value of the food. If the food came from the money earned by corruption, or as wages of crime or some other kind of dishonest act, it will reflect in the nature and character of the offspring, the descendents of the eater. It is not a medically proven fact. But the people have found the theory to be correct in their own experience.

वित्तं देहि गुणान्वितेषु मतिमन्नान्यत्र देहि क्वचित्
प्राप्तं वारिनिधेर्जलं घनमुखे माधुर्ययुक्तं सदा।
जीवान्स्थावरजङ्गमांश्च सकलान् संजीव्य भूमण्डलम्।
भूयः पश्य तदेव कोटिगुणितं गच्छन्तमम्भोनिधिम्।।

O God, give riches to the noble people only. Not to others. The saline water of the seas becomes pure water through cloud formation. The clouds rain water on land to give life to all living land creatures and vegetation. Then it goes back to the seas. (4)

Whatever any bad aspect money may have, in the hands of the noble people it will get purified. Because they will invest the money in good causes, charity and other noble deeds. Just like sea water turning into clouds of pure water vapours. The money so invested will benefit everyone of the society like rain water. The money in the hands of the bad people will only generate evils of crime and immorality.

चाण्डालानां सहस्रे च सूरिभिस्तत्त्वदर्शिभिः।
एको हि यवनः प्रोक्तो न नीचो यवनात् परः।।

Sages says that one Yavana, the foreign invader is as filthy as thousand scavengers. (5)

Here, Chanakya has spewed his venom against foreign invaders. It was the time when the alien invaders had begun raiding and trampling our land. His feeling of hatred is understandable.

तैलाऽभ्यंगे चिताधूमे मैथुने क्षौरकर्मणि।
तावद्भवति चाण्डालो यावत्स्नानं न चाऽऽचरेत्।।

A person is dirty until he has thoroughly washed himself after; oil massage, attending a funeral, having sex and a hair cut. (6)

Simple meaning, no elaboration is required.

अजीर्णे भेषजं वारि जीर्णे वारि बलप्रदम्।
भोजने चामृतं वारि भोजनान्ते विषप्रदम्।।

In case of indigestion, the water is medicine. After digestion is cured water gives strength. It is as good as nectar if taken little by little during the course of meals. Then after the meals water is poison. (7)

Chanakya dabbled in medicines as well. He had worked out his own theories. His theory about water is curious. We have seen people drinking water after taking meals and suffering no ill-effects. We shall leave it to the professionals to put in a word.

हतं ज्ञानं क्रियाहीनं हतश्चाऽज्ञानतो नरः।
हतं निर्नायकं सैन्यं स्त्रियो नष्टा ह्यभर्तृकाः।।

The education or learning is purposeless if it is not put to practical use, a sheer waste. An uneducated person is a wasted life. An army gets wasted without a general. Similarly a woman without a husband is a shameful waste. (8)

No elaboration is required.

वृद्धकाले मृता भार्या बन्धुहस्ते गतं धनम्।
भोजनं च पराधीनं तिस्रः पुंसां विडम्बनाः।।

Great tragedy befalls a man; whose wife passes away in old age, whose money is usurped by cousins and who depends on others for food. (9)

Old age is the stage when a man badly needs the wife to keep company with. The friends are no more there. The family member neglect him and consider him as a burden. The life long toil to feed the family shows up on his body as variety of ailments and weakness. The wife is the only one who knows his story of sacrifices and understands him. In her death old man's soul dies. The money and the wealth gone to cousins never comes back. The only things the cousins give are threats and abuses.

नाग्निहोत्रं विना वेदा न च दानं विना क्रिया।
न भावेन विना सिद्धिस्तस्माद्भावो हि कारणम्।।

Studying Vedas without performing yagna is worthless. Yagna without charity is useless. A fully committed spirit is essential for any religious act. (10)

Without full devotion, sincere faith and committed spirit no religious act fructifies. A half done act is worse than not done.

91

काष्ठपाषाणधातूनां कृत्वा भावेन सेवनम् ।
श्रद्धया च तया सिद्धस्तस्य विष्णुः प्रसीदति ।।

A God idol of wood, stone or a metal should be worshipped only with the firm faith that God is present in it. The God blesses according to the worshippers' faith. (11)

An idol in itself is just a stone or lump of a metal. It becomes representative of God only when a devotee projects his own faith in the idol. Hence a worshipper gets blessed in the ratio of his faith.

न देवो विद्यते काष्ठे न पाषाणे न मृन्मये ।
भावे हि विद्यते देवस्तस्माद् भावो हि कारणम् ।।

God and lords are not found in wooden or stone idols. They remain in the souls of human beings. It means where human pray god with full fair and devout, the god itself appear there. (12)

No elaboration is required.

शान्तितुल्यं तपो नास्ति न सन्तोषात्परं सुखम् ।
न तृष्णायाः परो व्याधिर्न च धर्मो दयापरः ।।

No blessing is greater than peace. No joy is greater than contentment. No desease is worse than greed. No religion is greater than mercy. (13)

The peace itself is earthly version of temporary state of *Nirvana. Nirvana* itself is nothing but eternal peace. Contentment is the purest form of happiness. The greed is the driving force of sin. Mercy, truly is the greatest of the good acts.

क्रोधो वैवस्वतो राजा तृष्णा वैतरणी नदी ।
विद्या कामदुधा धेनुः सन्तोषो नन्दनं वनम् ।।

Anger is death. Avarice is river of agony. Education is all providing and contendedness is the biggest blessing. (14)

Anger is a raging fire that burns a person's body without sending out flames. Too much greed ultimately drowns one in the river of woes. Education and contentment has already been commented upon.

गुणो भूषयते रूपं शीलं भूषयते कुलम्।
सिद्धिर्भूषयते विद्यां भोगो भूषयते धनम्।।

Good qualities enhance beauty, gentlemanliness gets credit to the family, practical implementation is tribute to learning and spending is honouring the money. (15)

If physical beauty is accompanied by good qualities it is like gold studded with jewels. The gentlemanliness and implementation of knowledge have been already commented upon. Spending money is truely appreciating the worth of it. It is made for spending. It can make life really enjoyable and can buy one all the comforts. A miser who does not spend money is like one who has a TV but does not watch programmes to save its 'brand new' status.

निर्गुणस्य हतं रूपं दुःशीलस्य हतं कुलम्।
असिद्धस्य हता विद्या अभोगेन हतं धनम्।।

A man of beauty without talents is worthless. An ill-mannered person shames the family. A man's learning without being put to practical use is waste. Money not spent is also useless. (16)

It is elaborated in earlier couplets.

शुचिर्भूमिगतं तोयं शुद्धा नारी पतिव्रता।
शुचिः क्षेमकरो राजा सन्तोषी ब्राह्मणः शुचिः।।

Water springing out of the ground is pure. A faithful wife is pious. A king who cares for his subjects is also pious. A contented Brahmin too is pious. (17)

93

Ground water is no more pure as it used to be. Today surface pollution has percolated down to the underground water table and polluted it. Now what springs up is impotable water. A faithful wife, caring king and contented Brahmin being pious are repetitions. Here one question arises that, is being faithful only woman's duty? Suppose, the man is not faithful and he passes on VD or AIDs to his wife. Shall we still call the wife pious? What would have Chanakya said?

असन्तुष्टा द्विजा नष्टाः सन्तुष्टाश्च महीभृतः ।
सलज्जा गणिका नष्टा निर्लज्जाश्च कुलाङ्गनाः ।।

An uncontent Brahmin, content king, a coy prostitute and shameless women from good families destroy themselves. (18)

An uncontent Brahmin would defraud his clients in religious matters and condemn himself. A content king would do no efforts to improve things in his state and let things drift to his downfall. A coy prostitute would ruin her business. The shameless women from good homes would sooner or later go astray and meet their doom.

किं कुलेन विशालेन विद्याहीनेन देहिनाम् ।
दुष्कुलीनोऽपि विद्वांश्च देवैरपि सुपूज्यते ।।

A great dynasty is no great if it is bereft of educated members. If a person of low birth gains learning and wisdom, he would be honourable for nobles even. (19)

A persons birth or origin is immaterial. What is important is that what he has made of himself? If someone has worked hard and risen to the great heights of learning and wisdom, all others should look up at him and admire. From which depths he rose up does not matter. And who would respect a supposedly great family if it has just a crowd of uneducated idiots to show?

विद्वान् प्रशस्यते लोके विद्वान् गच्छति गौरवम् ।
विद्यया लभते सर्वं विद्या सर्वत्र पूज्यते ।।

The world respects the wise ones, the scholars. The wise ones get honoured and rewarded with riches. One can get anything through learning. It is worshipped everywhere. (20)

मांसभक्षैः सुरापानैर्मूर्खैश्चाक्षरवर्जितैः ।
पशुभिः पुरुषाकारैर्भाराऽऽक्रान्ता च मेदिनी ।।

This earth is in agony of being crushed by the heavy burden of animal humans in the form of; flesh eater, drunkards, idiots and uneducated. (21)

अन्नहीनो दहेद् राष्ट्रं मन्त्रहीनश्च ऋत्विजः ।
यजमानं दानहीनो नास्ति यज्ञसमो रिपुः ।।

A yajna is enemy like if it; empties the food coffers of the country, is being conducted by ritualistic priests who don't know the meaning of mantras or the organisers of which are strangers to charity. (22)

Chanakya is perhaps lamenting against the big yajnas where large amounts of food grains and *ghee* was burnt in fire while people all around starved. Streams of milk were poured into the rivers while children went without milk. How could such wasteful exercises create goodwill and prosperity for all? Perhaps the greedy priests and pompous organisers never understood the spirit of yajna.

The Summary of the Chapter

High class people work only for honour and recognition while the low class only cared for money.

The money is not to be kept idle. It must be invested in good deeds and projects. There is no harm if someone honours the money by using it to have a good life. The idea is to keep the money circulating.

Tragedy is the death of the wife of an old man, who has lost her when he wanted her most becuase she was the only one who understood him and cared for him.

Idols are merely pieces of stone, wood or metal. No God lives in them. They become worshippable only when a devotee projects his own faith into them. Hence, the blessing granted is in the ratio of the faith of the worshipper.

A person of low birth also becomes honourable if he educates himself to reach the heights of learning and wisdom. A high family if it fails to show educated amongst its members then it does not deserve to be called a high family.

The flesh eaters, drunkards, idiots and persons of no education are burden on this earth.

A yajna that burns away the food stocks of the country is enemy like. The organisers and priests of such yajnas are ignorant fools who neither understand the meaning of mantras nor they have true spirit.

Peace is the greatest blessing and contentedness is biggest joy.

❏❏

CHAPTER NINE

Do not wake up; The king, serpant, tiger, pig, child, other's dog and a fool. Leave them asleep.

मुक्तिमिच्छसि चेत्तात विषयान् विषवत् त्यज ।
क्षमाऽऽर्जवं दया शौचं सत्यं पीयूषवद् भज ।।

If you wish for deliverence, give up bad habits and bad addictions considering them poison. Partake the nectar of forgiveness, tolerance, patience, piety and the truth. (1)

Bad habits and bad addictions are openings through which bigger evils keep entering into a person. In a short time the person becomes a houseful of sins having gradually displaced all the goodness. Salvation becomes impossible. The qualities of tolerance, patience, piety etc. are seeds which yield a harvest of goodness.

परस्परस्य मर्माणि ये भाषन्ते नराधमाः ।
त एवं विलयं यान्ति वल्मीकोदरसर्पवत् ।।

Those who reveal the secrets of others and use foul language, they got destroyed like a snake trapped in a mothhill perishes. (2)

Betraying a friend by revealing his secret to others is the most lowly and condemnable act. It just shows how low he has fallen. Nothing can redeem such person. Naturally, persons who degrade themselves to such depth will only speak harsh and abusive language. The end is never far.

गन्धः सुवर्णे फलमिक्षुदण्डे
नाऽकारि पुष्पं खलु चन्दनस्य।
विद्वान् धनाढ्यश्च नृपश्चिरायुः
धातुः पुरा कोऽपि न बुद्धिदोऽभूत्।।

Brahma, the creator, did not bestow; fragrance to gold, sweet fruit to sugarcane plant and flowers to sandalwood tree. Neither did he grant riches to a scholar or long life to the king. It appears the creator had no wise advisor. (3)

Chanakya here is lamenting the folly of the creator Brahma for not granting riches to the scholars. The trouble is that in ancient India most of the Brahmins passed off as scholars who were infact insult to the learning. They were barely literate who just about managed to mumble a few Sanskrit couplets or quatrains. And they all lived on alms. How could they become rich? A country or a society, produces only a few real scholars at a time. But here we had a situation where entire mob of Brahmins wanted every member of its ilk to be accepted as professional scholar!

सर्वोषधीनाममृता प्रधाना सर्वेषु सौख्येष्वशनं प्रधानम्।
सर्वेन्द्रियाणां नयनं प्रधानं सर्वेषु गात्रेषु शिरः प्रधानम्।।

Nectar is the king of all the medicines. The food is the most satisfying of all means of pleasure. Eye is the queen of all the sensory organs. Head is the most superior of all the parts of the body. (4)

दूतो न सञ्चरति खे न चलेच्च वार्ता
पूर्वं न जल्पितमिदं न च सङ्गमोऽस्ति।
व्योम्नि स्थितं रविशशिग्रहणं प्रशस्तं
जानाति यो द्विजवरः स कथं न विद्वान्।।

It is not possible to send a spy to the skies. No one can send any message to the earthlings from the skies. So, why shouldn't the Brahmins who correctly predict the timings of the eclipse of sun or moon every year be considered scholars? (5)

With due apologies, here again we differ with Chanakya. Just as we doubted the scholarly qualifications of Brahmins while commenting on the quatrain-3, this quatrain supports our stand unwittingly. Brahma did not need an advisor, what infact is needed is to define clearly the meaning of the scholar. Ability to read a few couplets should not qualify one to be taken as a great scholar as the Brahmins wanted. Here guru Chanakya also is demanding the same because some Brahmins predicted timings of solar and lunar eclipses in Almanacs. The fact is that predicting eclipse timings is no scholarly pursuit. It is merely a mathematical calculation. One only needs to know the formula to do it. Today, tens of millions of students of schools can do it.

विद्यार्थी सेवकः पान्थः क्षुधाऽऽर्तो भयकातरः।
भाण्डारी प्रतिहारी च सप्त सुप्तान् प्रबोधयेत्।।

The student, the servant, the traveller, the starving person and the guard be woken up if found sleeping at duty. (6)

The student has to resume reading as he has fallen asleep in the process of studying. The traveller has miles to go as his tired body oversleeps. A starving person must look for food or he will never wake up. A guard must keep vigil.

अहिं नृपं च शार्दूलं किटिं च बालकं तथा।
परश्वानं च मूर्खं च सप्त सुप्तान् न बोधयेत्।।

Don't ever wake up a sleeping; serpent, king, tiger, pig, child, other's dog and fool. Leave them asleep. (7)

The above can cause harm to the one who foolishly tries to wake them up. The serpant and the dog, will bite. The king and the tiger will maul in anger. The child will start bawling and it will be impossible to quieten him down. The pig will go foraging to annoy everyone. A fool awoken will do more foolish acts and land himself in trouble.

अर्थाऽधीताश्च यैर्वेदास्तथा शूद्रान्नभोजिनाः।
ते द्विजाः किं करिष्यन्ति निर्विषा इव पन्नगाः।।

The Brahmins who study scriptures to make money and seek alms from lowly people lose respect of others. The people will withdraw their faith in him making him like poisonless snake. (8)

A poisonless snake does not inspire any awe. A priest also needs to inspire some awe to command the faith of the faithful.

यस्मिन् रुष्टे भयं नास्ति तुष्टे नैव धनाऽऽगमः।
निग्रहोऽनुग्रहो नास्ति स रुष्टः किं करिष्यति।।

One whose anger inspires no awe, whose getting pleased results in no gain and one whose authority can pass no punishment or grant any reward; are of no consequence. (9)

One can command the attention of people only if one has some power to influence the fate of others physically or spiritually. A powerless person is like a toothless lion who gradually perishes due to ineffectiveness.

निर्विषेणाऽपि सर्पेण कर्तव्या महती फणा।
विषमस्तु न चाप्यस्तु घटाटोपो भयङ्करः।।

*Even a poisonless snake must raise its hood to frighten
away the enemy because the enemy does not know about the
absence of poison in it. (10)*

There is no harm in using deterrent in self defence. The
nature also uses this trick. In animal kingdom numerous
creatures adopt this tactic to deal with the enemy. Snorting,
barking, showing teeth, puffing feathers or body, snarling
and making scary sounds are part of the same game. The
nuclear deterrent serves the same purpose. The cardgame
gamblers call it bluffing.

प्रातर्द्यूतप्रसंगेन   मध्याह्ने   स्त्रीप्रसङ्गतः।
रात्रौ चौर्यप्रसंगेन कालो गच्छत्यधीमताम्।।

*The wise men spend their time in reading; the story of
gamblers in the morning, the drama of women during the day
and the adventures of thiefs at the night. (11)*

This couplet has been written in lighter vein. The story
of gamblers means 'Mahabharata' in which the gambling
habit of Pandava King Yudhishthira served as the main plot
to build up the saga. The drama of women refers to 'Ramayana'
where acts of the queen Kaikayee and Sita's obstinacy
provide the scripts for the epic. The adventures of thief is
pointer to Geeta, the creation of Lord Kirshna, the thief of
butter and the hearts of maidens. Some scholars interpret the
above couplet as following:

Fools waste their mornings in gambling, the days in
romancing and the nights in stealing.

स्वहस्तग्रथिता   माला   स्वहस्तघृष्टचन्दनम्।
स्वहस्तलिखितं स्तोत्रं शक्रस्यापि श्रियं हरेत्।।

Offering to God a self made garland, applying sandal wood paste made by own hands and singing self-written prayer, earns one the riches of the heavens as reward from God. (12)

One should worship God with his own efforts instead of getting it done through priests or Brahmins as a contract job. That seems to be the message. And the reward promised appears to be merely an advertisement gimmick.

इक्षुदण्डास्तिलाः क्षुद्राः कान्ता हेम च मेदिनी ।
चन्दनं दधि ताम्बूलं मर्दनं गुणवर्धनम् ।।

Cane, oilseed, fool, lowly person, woman, gold, land, sandalwood, curd and paan; these are the things which become better and better as one gives them more and more rubdowns and shake-downs. (13)

The above tips might appear unpalatable to a modern mind as times and situations have drastically changed. Especially in the case of fool, woman and the lowly person. They are no more considered only fit for stick and rebuke.

दरिद्रता धीरतया विराजते कुवस्त्रता शुभ्रतया विराजते ।
कदन्नता चोष्णतया विराजते कुरूपता शीलतया विराजते ।।

In poverty, the patience makes the poverty bearable. Even an ordinary piece of cloth looks good if kept clean. If food is not rich and tasty, eating it fresh and hot makes it tolerable. Similarly a good character makes up for the lack of physical beauty. (14)

What can not be cured must be endured. There are simple ways to make it endurable. The patience and stoicism can help tide over the difficult period. What is important is to keep hold on positive attitude.

The Summary of the Chapter

If one desires salvation, the first thing one should do is to give up bad habits and addictions. Replace them with forgiveness, patience, forebearance and the truth.

A betrayer of confidence is the worst kind of person. Such person eventually leads to his own downfall. In the chapter, some debatable issues have arisen. It appears that Chanakya wants the people who have little learning to be accepted as scholars. The knowledge to read a few mantras can't make one a person of learning. He contends that since Brahmins can predict solar and lunar eclipse, they should be recognised as scholars on the strength of this ability alone. But it is not a scholarly achievement. Today millions of students of mathematics can do it easily by using a simple formula. Any one can work out timings of eclipses for the coming centuries even by using that table.

Use of deterrence in self defence is natural. Even the animals employ this trick to avoid actual battle. Some power is needed to influence the mind of others. It can be physical power, power of authority to punish or reward or psychological power. Such powers inspire awe in masses or enemies. The kings and authorities have power to punish others or give rewards. Hence, they command respect of the people. A religious leader has psychological power over devotees by posing as representative of the awe inspiring power of God. The elephants inspire awe through their sheer size. The snakes and big cats have strange mesmerising power. That is in addition to their physical power to kill others.

A student, servant, traveller, straving man and a guard must stay awake to do their task. But the king, snake, tiger, pig, child, other's dog and fool must be allowed to sleep. If awoken they can inflict harm or create troubles.

❏❏

CHAPTER TEN

Poets can imagine anything. Women can do anything. A drunkard can say anything. And a crow can eat anything.

धनहीनो न हीनश्च धनिकः स सुनिश्चयः।
विद्यारत्नेन यो हीनः स हीनः सर्ववस्तुषु।।

A moneyless man is not poor if he has got the riches of learning. A man who has no learning is the poorest, even if he has money. (1)

This thought is a poor consolation for a penniless man of learning. Because in the practical life some money is needed for daily survivial.

दृष्टिपूतं न्यसेत् पादं वस्त्रपूतं पिबेज्जलम्।
शास्त्रपूतं वदेद् वाक्यं मनः पूतं समाचरेत्।।

A man must tread with his eyes open, drink filtered water, say some educated thing and do any task only after giving it a careful thought. (2)

No elaboration is required.

सुखार्थी वा त्यजेद्विद्यां विद्यार्थी वा त्यजेत् सुखम्।
सुखार्थिनः कुतो विद्या विद्यार्थिनः कुतो सुखम्।।

If you wish for comforts then forget about education. A student who wants to learn must give up comforts. There is no scope for it. (3)

In middle ages Indian educational institutions were run on different lines. A student's life was very tough and disciplined. The teachers worked on the theory that stick and rebuke were right tools of education. The more a student was beaten and humiliated, the more he would learn, they thought. No luxuries were allowed. Even essentials were denied to them. The students were given very little to eat and little to wear. They were nothing better than prisoners. It was thought that such sort of denials and sufferings were good for the student's learning process. It was a torture. Very few students survived this system.

May be, it was good for the students. Because there were little opportunities for the learned people. He would starve as a scholar and live like a beggar any way. The schools trained students for it.

कवयः किं न पश्यन्ति किं न कुर्वन्ति योषितः ।
मद्यपाः किं न जल्पन्ति किं न भक्षन्ति वायसाः ।।

Poets can imagine anything. Women can do anything. A drunkard can say anything. A crow can eat anything. (4)

Women doing anything needs comments. Actually the daredevilry shown by women was merely desperate acts. The women were denied their rights, or nobody thought they could have any human rights. Rigorous restrictions and cruel conditions were forced on them by the society. The doors of justice were closed to women and lower castes. Even after a great ordeal a woman failed to get a small justice even. The society was deaf and blind to them. So, some women tried to defy society in desparate situations. And the people said that women can do anything.

रङ्कं करोति राजानं राजानं रङ्कमेव च।
धनिनं निर्धनं चैव निर्धनं धनिनं विधिः।।

The fate and God is great. A beggar can become a king in a jiffy if the two liked. And a king can be reduced to a beggar. A rich man becomes poor and, a poor becomes rich! (5)

No need to elaborate.

लुब्धानां याचकः शत्रुर्मूर्खाणां बोधकः रिपुः।
जारस्त्रीणां पतिः शत्रुश्चोराणां चन्द्रमा रिपुः।।

A greedy person's enemy is beggar. A fool's enemy is one who gives him wise advice. A flirt woman's enemy is her husband. And the thief's enemy is moon. (6)

A beggar's appearance angers the greedy because the greedy never gives anything to any one. So, beggar is his enemy. A fool has no use for good advice. For a flirt her husband is a hinderance. And the moon sheds light to make things difficult for a thief.

येषां न विद्या न तपो न दानं न ज्ञानं न शीलं न गुणो न धर्मः।
ते मर्त्यलोके भुवि भारभूता मनुष्यरूपेण मृगाश्चरन्ति।।

Animals are those people; who have no learning, who have never done penance, who are not charitable, who have no skill, no politeness and no mercy. They are beasts in human form. (7)

Elaboration is not required.

अन्तःसारविहीनानामुपदेशो न जायते।
मलयाचलसंसर्गात् न वेणुश्चन्दनायते।।

It is of no use to give wise advice to persons who have no capacity to receive or imbibe. The fragrant winds coming from the forest of sandalwood trees do not aromate the bamboo groves which continue to be offensive smelling. (8)

No elaboration is required.

यस्य नास्ति स्वयं प्रज्ञा शास्त्रं तस्य करोति किम्।
लोचनाभ्यां विहीनस्य दर्पणः किं करिष्यति।।

What can holy books do to a person who has no brains?
What will a blind man do with a mirror? (9)

The Vedas and other holy books are useless for a
thoughless person as the mirror solves no purpose for a
blind.

दुर्जनं सज्जनं कर्तुमुपायो न हि भूतले।
अपानं शतधा धौतं न श्रेष्ठमिन्द्रियं भवेत्।।

There is no way in this world which can turn an evil
person into a gentleman. Wishing anus a hundred times in a
hundred ways won't make it desirable as the mouth. (10)

Chanakya had a very special revulsion for evil people or
bad characters. He has ridiculed and condemned them a
hundred times in a hundred ways.

आत्मद्वेषात् भवेन्मृत्युः परद्वेषात् धनक्षयः।
राजद्वेषात् भवेन्नाशो ब्रह्मद्वेषात् कुलक्षयः।।

One who is in conflict with his own soul, perishes. One
who is in conflict with learned, sages and noble souls, also
perishes. Having conflict with others causes destruction of
own wealth. One who is in conflict with the king, causes his
own perishment. Being in conflict with Brahmins results in
perishment of the whole dynasty. (11)

Here Chanakya is displaying his partisan attitude in
favour of his own Brahmin class. He is warning everyone that
whoever crosses the path of Brahmins will face disaster.

वरं वनं व्याघ्रगजेन्द्रसेवितं द्रुमालयं पत्रफलाम्बुभोजनम्।
तृणेषु शय्या शतजीर्णवल्कलं न बन्धुमध्ये धनहीनजीवनम्।।

Better live in a jungle infested with violent beasts like
lions and tigers, better live on wild berries, tree leaves and

water, better sleep on the bed of pine needles, better wear fig leaves; but don't ever live with your kith and kin when poverty strikes you. (12)

A poor relative is a picture of misery. Every one derives some pleasure in insulting and humiliating him. He loses his self-respect in a few seconds if he goes to live on the mercy of his kith and kin. The every sentence they speak would be barbed with sarcasm. The snide remarks would pierce him. The food served would be poisoned with open contempt. The hardships of a jungle would appear kinder in comparison.

विप्रो वृक्षस्तस्य मूलं च सन्ध्या
वेदाः शाखा धर्मकर्माणि पत्रम् ।
तस्मान्मूलं यत्नतो रक्षणीयं
छिन्ने मूले नैव शाखा न पत्रम् ।।

Brahmin is a tree. The service to God is the roots of the tree. The scriptures are its branches. The religious rites and other rituals are its leaves. So, protect the roots with great care. If the roots get destroyed the tree will fall down. (13)

Chanakya is advising his Brahmin brotheren to keep in the service of God with all devotion and visibility. Because it sustains the Brahmin-hood, provides them with food and other essentials, keeps the masses in their awe and gives them all the psychological advantages.

माता च कमलादेवी पिता देवो जनार्दनः ।
बान्धवा विष्णुभक्ताश्च स्वदेशो भुवनत्रयम् ।।

All the worlds are home for one; whose mother is goddess Laxmi, father is Lord Vishnu, and brothers are all the faithfuls. (14)

एकवृक्षसमारूढा नाना वर्णा विहङ्गमाः ।
प्रभाते दशसु दिक्षु तत्र का परिवेदना ।।

The birds of several species, shapes, sizes and colours converge on a tree in the evening to spend the night. In the morning all fly away in different directions. In the same way all relatives come together in a family and then go their ways when the time comes. Why grieve for one another on separation? (15)

The people come together to make family or a circle of friends and then one by one they depart compelled by different reasons. Every one has own life to live with own plans. That is the fact of life. The separation from one another should not be turned into a life long sorrow. Give due respect to the nature's law.

बुद्धिर्यस्य बलं तस्य निर्बुद्धेस्तु कुतो बलम्।
वने सिंहो मदोन्मत्तः शशकेन निपातितः।।

Brain power is the mightiest power. The physical power may look fearsome but it has no clever edge to win against wisdom. Remember the story how a lion got killed by a clever rabbit. (16)

The reference is to a story from Panchatantra in which a clever rabbit leads an angered lion on a ploy to a well and tricks it jumping into the well to meet its death. Thus the rabbit outwitted the mighty lion using his brain.

का चिन्ता मम जीवने यदि हरिर्विश्वम्भरो गीयते
नो चेदर्भकजीवनाय जननीस्तन्यं कथं निर्मयेत्।
इत्यालोच्य मुहुर्मुहुर्युदुपते लक्ष्मीपते केवलं
त्वत्पादाम्बुजसेवनेन सततं कालो मया नीयते।।

Lord Vishnu is supposed to be the provider of the world. If it's true then I don't have anything to worry. He arranges milk in the breasts of the mother for the child who still is in the womb. So thinking, O Lord of the Universe, I spend my life serving you. (17)

It is a kind of prayer Chanakya is making to God. He, being the provider, Chanakya believes, He will arrange something for his sustainance also while he devotes his time singing His praises.

गीर्वाणवाणीषु विशिष्टबुद्धिस्तथापि भाषान्तरलोलुपोऽहम् ।
यथा सुराणाममृते स्थितेऽपि स्वर्गाङ्गनानामधरासवे रुचिः ॥

I am hungry from other languages too besides Sanskrit. Similarly as the gods of the heaven thirst for the lips of the heavenly beauties even after partaking the nectar. (18)

Mythological belief is that the gods and demons churned the sea out of which emerged a pitcherful of nectar. The gods managed to corner the pitcher and drank the nectar. These gods live in heaven under Lord Indra as their king. The heavenly beauties are called *Apsaras* who serve as hostesses of the Indra's court.

अन्नाद्दशगुणं पिष्टं पिष्टाद्दशगुणं पयः ।
पयसोऽष्टगुणं मांसं मांसाद्दशगुणं घृतम् ॥

The flour has ten times more nutritional value than the grains. Milk has ten times more value than the floor. Meat has eight times more value than the milk. And Ghee has ten times more energy value than the meat. (19)

The doctors do not agree with this theory.

शाकेन रोगा वर्धन्ते पयसा वर्धते तनुः ।
घृतेन वर्धते वीर्यं मांसान्मांसं प्रवर्धते ॥

The leafy vegetables breed deseases. The milk fattens the body. The ghee builds up semen. And the meat adds meat only. (20)

This couplet again is in conflict with the modern medical science. The doctors advise us to eat more fibrous leafy vegetables. They think little of ghee which only is concentrated fat, according to them.

The Summary of the Chapter

Animals are those people who have not received any education. And those who are not compassionate, no skill for anything and those who know not what charity is. A person who has got knowledge or skill for something, is richer than the rich who is not educated.

One must look carefully before treading to avoid ditches or potholes. A project needs careful thought before being started.

To benefit from someone's advice a person must have capacity to imbibe or receive. A seive collects no water. No book can help a slow brain. A mirror in the hands of a blind person is of no use.

Don't ever live with your relatives as a poor consin. It will kill your self respect and you will lose confidence in yourself. It would be better to retreat to some jungle and face its dangers. There you may lose your life but the honour will remain intact.

The birds converge on a tree in the evening to spend the night. But in the morning all of them fly in different directions in search of food. Man must learn a lesson from this. People come together and then they go their own ways to pursue their own interest. The separations must not grieve you. It is a law of nature.

The brain power is greater than brawn power. The brain has the winning edge.

Then there are tips on diets and nutritional food values from Chanakya which do not confirm to the theories of the modern medical science. May be, it is because of the different situations and different needs of the people of today.

❑❑

CHAPTER ELEVEN

A person who maintains silence for one year, opening his mouth only to eat, he gets all the honours of the heaven for ten million years.

दातृत्वं प्रियवक्तृत्वं धीरत्वमुचितज्ञता।
अभ्यासेन न लभ्यन्ते चत्वारः सहजा गुणाः॥

There are four natural propensities in people; for charity, polite talk, stoicism and basic logic. These can not be grafted or created. (1)

These qualities are there in one's nature in raw state in the beginning. These can not be grafted or imported. But surely they have to be nursed to bring them up from the dormant state. And then they have to be polished. That is what the education process does. For example, in the case of the polite talk, one has to learn right type of language and practise the delivery.

आत्मवर्गं परित्यज्य परवर्गं समाश्रयेत्।
स्वयमेव लयं याति यथा राजाऽन्यधर्मतः॥

A man who goes to join another community leaving his

own, perishes in no time just like a person who converts to another religion. Similarly a king perishes who gives up his basic duty of protecting his subjects. (2)

A person gone to another community rarely gets acceptance. It takes generations to get the acceptance. For the first generation convert the doubts and suspicions dog him. The people of adopted community or religion remain sceptic to the newcomer's motives. His character carries a question mark always. Just as a politician who defects from one party to another is seldom respected. Such person is bound to suffer in personal and professional life.

हस्ती स्थूलतनुः स चाङ्कुशवशः किं हस्तिमात्रोङ्कुशो
दीपे प्रज्वलिते प्रणश्यति तमः किं दीपमात्रं तमः।
वज्रेणापि हताः पतन्ति गिरयः किं वज्रमात्रो गिरिम्
तेजो यस्य विराजते स बलवान् स्थूलेषु कः प्रत्ययः।।

An elephant is giant in size but a small goad keeps it under control. A small lamp destroys a huge amount of darkness. A mountain can be broken down with repeated blows of a small hammer. Are a goad, a lamp and a hammer any match to the elephant, darkness and the mountain in size respectively? (3)

The size does not matter. It is the power, potential and the quality of a thing that matters.

कलौ दशसहस्रेषु हरिस्त्यजति मेदिनीम्।
तदर्थं जाह्नवीतोयं तदर्थं ग्रामदेवता।।

It is believed that God deserts the earth after ten thousand years of Kaliyuga (The age of evil). After five thousand years of the same the holy waters of the river Ganges desert the earth. After 2500 years the deity of the village departs from there. (4)

It is some mythological belief contained in some scripture. And the message too is not clear.

गृहाऽऽसक्तस्य नो विद्या नो दया मांसभोजिनः।
द्रव्यलुब्धस्य नो सत्यं स्त्रैणस्य न पवित्रता।।

A student who remains homesick learns nothing. People who eat flesh have no mercy. Persons who have greed for money are no truthful. And one who is a debauch can not attain piety. (5)

A homesick student naturally won't be able to concentrate on studies. The meat can not inspire mercy because it itself is a product of the extreme act of cruelty, the killing. And of course, the wealth is the most glorious product of the greed. One can not make money without resorting the various kinds of false statements in the course of the business. Truthfulness will only result in all the earnings going to the government in the form of the taxes, that's the bottomline.

न दुर्जनः साधुदशामुपैति बहुप्रकारैरपि शिक्ष्यमाणः।
आमूलसिक्तः पयसा घृतेन न निम्बवृक्षो मधुरत्वमेति।।

A Neem tree does not taste sweet even if it is irrigated with milk and butter. Similarly no amount of advice and counselling can turn an evil person into a noble one. (6)

The basic nature is impossible to change.

अन्तर्गतमलो   दुष्टस्तीर्थस्नानशतैरपि।
न शुध्यति यथा भाण्डं सुराया दाहितं च यत्।।

No amount of pilgrimage and temple going can redeem a person whose mind is filled with evil desires. Similarly, as a wine container does not become clean even after going through the fire of a furnace. (7)

It shows Chanakya's strong disapproval of the drinking. He has compared the container of liquor to a person of evil mind, the incorrigible.

न वेत्ति यो यस्य गुणप्रकर्षं
स तं सदा निन्दति नाऽत्र चित्रम्।
यथा किराती करिकुम्भजाता
मुक्ताः परित्यज्य बिभर्ति गुञ्जाः ।।

Anyone of little knowledge and little evaluation power, trying to belittle a learned person, is no surprise. A foolish tribal woman, ignores the pearls and adorns herself with cheap beads. (8)

Here, Chanakya leaves nothing more to be said. So well illustrated, it is!

ये तु संवत्सरं पूर्णं नित्यं मौनेन भुञ्जते।
युगकोटिसहस्रं तु स्वर्गलोके महीयते।।

A person who keeps silence for one whole year, opening the mouth only to eat food, gets all the honours of the heaven for ten million years. (9)

'The heaven's honours for the ten million years' is merely a figure of speech used to convey the importance of the silence. His way of saying 'The silence is gold' but adding more value to it.

कामं क्रोधं तथा लोभं स्वादं शृङ्गारकौतुके।
अतिनिद्राऽतिसेवे च विद्यार्थी ह्यष्ट वर्जयेत्।।

A true student of education must refrain from; love, anger, infatuation, delicacies, preening, the entertainment shows, oversleeping and flattery. (10)

All other refrains are logical except the last one about flattery. It can be implied in two ways. One is that the flattery by the fellow students can make one a vain person which will do no good. The other is that the student who becomes a flatterer harms his studies ruining his own career. The flattery of teachers might pass him in the exams but he will do no real learning which will show in later life.

अकृष्टफलमूलेन वनवासरतः सदा।
कुरुतेऽहरहः श्राद्धमृषिर्विप्रः स उच्यते।।

A Brahmin who lives on the produce of the natural wilderness (Uncultivated land), lives happily in the jungle and performs religious rites everyday, is a sage. (11)

एकाहारेण सन्तुष्टः षट्कर्मनिरतः सदा।
ऋतुकालाभिगामी च स विप्रो द्विज उच्यते।।

One who eats only one meal a day to keep the body and the mind safe from the evils of excess feeding, does his everyday duties religiously, mates with his wife to sire offspring and not for pleasure; such a person is the true Brahmin. (12)

Here 'Brahmin' is descriptive of a model of physically, morally and spiritually correct person.

लौकिके कर्मणि रतः पशूनां परिपालकः।
वाणिज्यकृषिकर्ता यः स विप्रो वैश्य उच्यते।।

A Brahmin who is involved in worldly activities, who raises cattle, does business or engages in agricultural work, is a mercenary Brahmin. Not a religious one. (13)

लाक्षादितैलनीलानां कुसुम्भमधुसर्पिषाम्।
विक्रेता मद्यमांसानां स विप्रः शूद्र उच्यते।।

A Brahmin who trades in lac products, oil, indigo, flowers, honey, wine, meat etc. is the lowest class of Brahmin. (14)

परकार्यविहन्ता च दाम्भिकः स्वार्थसाधकः।
छली द्वेषी मृदुः क्रूरो विप्रो मार्जार उच्यते।।

One who spoils the works of others, who is egoistic, self-serving, treacherous and jealous covertly but who tries to overtly show himself as a very polite and honest character, such a Brahmin is a cat. (15)

According to our mythological beliefs, the cat is a lowly creature. Its character is symbolic of deceit, greed and stealth.

वापी-कूप-तडागानामाराम-सुर-वेश्मनाम्
उच्छेदने निराऽऽशङ्कः स विप्रो म्लेच्छ उच्यते।।

A Brahmin who desecrates any source of water, spring well, well, pond, gardens and parks or temples without any hesitation, is called lowly infidel. (16)

देवद्रव्यं गुरुद्रव्यं परदाराऽभिमर्शनम्।
निर्वाहः सर्वभूतेषु विप्रश्चाण्डाल उच्यते।।

One who steals from temples or from guru, who uses wives of others and who lives with all kinds of animals, is called charlatan. (17)

देयं भोज्यधनं सदा सुकृतिभिर्नो सञ्चितव्यं कदा
श्रीकर्णस्य बलेश्च विक्रमपतेर्द्यापि कीर्तिः स्थिता।
अस्माकं मधु दानभोगरहितं नष्टं चिरात्सञ्चितं
निर्वाणादिति पाणिपादयुगले घर्षन्त्यहो मक्षिकाः।।

The bees which collect honey with such exemplary courage and hard work, also have to repent if they don't give away some honey because it gets destroyed. Similarly people who amass wealth and don't put the money to good use like in charity, lose it in various ways. The kings and men of riches who generously gave away their money earned glory and fame that still survives. (18)

Too much stored honey attracts enemies like bears and other honey eating creatures leading to the destruction of the entire honeycomb. The hoarded money also invites plunderers.

The Summary of the Chapter

Those who leave their own flock to join the flock of the birds of different feathers don't flourish. They lose self-respect and seldom get any respect in the new company. They don't get a chance to settle down peacefully being suspect in the eyes of the others. This ultimately spells their doom.

This chapter contains a lot of thing specially written in respect of Brahmins, their duties and beliefs. It does not impart any great knowledge and thought. Hence, this part is merely dogmatic lecture or orthodox beliefs of little importance.

Great emphasis has been laid on charity. May be, because during the middle ages the entire Brahmin mob lived on the charity of the ruling, trading and landlord classes. The charity for Brahmins was sole means of survival. So, the above classes were exhorted every now and then to be charitable by dangling the carrot of the promised rewards in this life, in another life or in heaven. A lot of dubious gimmicks were inserted into original scriptures to propagate charity to Brahmins. Even Chanakya does not hesitate to become the part of that campaign.

The other reason was that economic management at governmental level was very poor or non-existent. A few people amassed all the wealth and the rest of the population just watched it helplessly. No viable taxation system was there to bring some economic parity and fairness in the society. The kings or rulers were not inclined to undertake any welfare works for the upliftment of the masses. Hence, charity was the only process which could chip some money off the wealthy people. Although it was not systematic or any productive way.

The only significant couplet in this chapter is which says that the physical size of a creature or a thing is not important. And that it is the quality, power and the potential that mattered. The examples given to prove this point are good.

❏ ❏

CHAPTER TWELVE

Drop by drop a pitcher gets filled. Similarly, a little by little collection of money, learning and good acts become great treasures.

सानन्दं सदनं सुताश्च सुधियः कान्ता प्रियालापिनी
इच्छापूर्तिधनं स्वयोषितिरतिः स्वाऽऽज्ञापराः सेवकाः।
आतिथ्यं शिवपूजनं प्रतिदिनं मिष्टान्नपानं गृहे
साधोः सङ्गमुपासते च सततं धन्यो गृहस्थाऽऽश्रमः।।

Blessed is a home where; the sons and daughters are obedient, the housewife is sweet tongued, the man is hard working, the money is wages of honesty, the friends are sincere, the wife is truly loved, the servants are faithful, the guests are welcome to overwhelming hospitality, God is worshipped, sweet dishes and refreshing drinks are always available and where holy teachers descend to provide enlightening discourses. (1)

आर्तेषु विप्रेषु दयान्वितश्च यत् श्रद्धया स्वल्पमुपैति दानम्।
अनन्तपारं समुपैति राजन् यद्दीयते तन्न लभेद् द्विजेभ्यः।।

O king, one who donates whatever with kindness and mercy to impoverished Brahmins, he is rewarded multiplied manifold in value by the Grace of God. (2)

Here, Chanakya is again championing the cause of the Brahmins by convassing liberal charity for them.

दाक्षिण्यं स्वजने दया परजने शाठ्यं सदा दुर्जने

प्रीतिः साधुजने स्मयः खलजने विद्वज्जने चार्जवम् ।

शौर्यं शत्रुजने क्षमा गुरुजने नारीजने धृष्टता

इत्थं ये पुरुषाः कलासु कुशलास्तेष्वेवलोकस्थितिः ।।

This world is kept going by the goodness of people who are polite and gentle to their near and dear ones, who deal with compassion to the deserving, show no mercy to bad people, who are respectful to the scholars, who bravely face the powerful, who display revernce to gurus, parents and spiritual teachers and who tackle women using cleverness instead of foolishly putting complete trust in them. (3)

हस्तौ दानविवर्जितौ श्रुतिपुटौ सारस्वतद्रोहिणौ

नेत्रे साधुविलोकनेन रहिते पादौ न तीर्थं गतौ ।

अन्यायार्जितवित्तपूर्णमुदरं गर्वेण तुंगं शिरो

रे रे जम्बुक मुञ्च मुञ्च सहसा निन्द्यं सुनिन्द्यं वपुः ।।

You whose hands are unaccustomed to the charity, whose ears never pay heed to the sermons of the holy scriptures, whose eyes never focus on saints, whose legs have not led the way to any pilgrimage centre, who has not looked after his parents or teachers, who has lived on the money earned through unjust means; O such man of over blown ego! You jackal like character! You are the lowliest of the low! You are condemnable. Leave that life of shame and spare this world! You are better dead than living! (4)

पत्रं नैव यदा करीरविटपे दोषो वसन्तस्य किं
नोलूकोऽप्यवलोकते यदि दिवा सूर्यस्य किं दूषणम्।
वर्षा नैव पतन्ति चातकमुखे मेघस्य किं दूषणं
यत्पूर्वं विधिना ललाटलिखितं तन्मार्जितुं कः क्षमः।।

If kareel tree does not grow leaves, is the spring to be blaimed? If the owl can't see during the day, is the sun to be blamed? If the rain drop does not fall into the open beak of the cuckoo, is cloud to be blamed? It is all in the fate, determined by the destiny. (5)

That what is written in fate, no power can erase it.

सत्सङ्गाद्भवति हि साधुता खलानां
साधूनां न हि खलसङ्गमात्खलत्वम्।
आमोदं कुसुम-भवं मृदेव धत्ते
मृद्गन्धं न हि कुसुमानि धारयन्ति।।

The company of a good person can inject goodness in a bad person. But the badness of the bad person never gets into the good man. Similarly as the fragrance of a flower can aromate the soil below but the musky smell of the soil never gets imbibed by the flower. (6)

साधूनां दर्शनं पुण्यं तीर्थभूता हि साधवः।
कालेन फलते तीर्थं सद्यः साधुसमागमः।।

Beholding a saintly man is a blessing because the saintly man is himself like a pilgrim centre. The pilgrimage brings good results only in a due course of time. But the sermons of a saintly men are the instant blessings. (7)

विप्राऽस्मिन्नगरे महान् कथय कस्तालद्रुमाणां गणः
को दाता रजको ददाति वसनं प्रातर्गृहीत्वा निशि।

को दक्षः परदारवित्तहरणे सर्वेऽपि दक्षो जनः
कस्माज्जीवसि हे सखे विषकृमिन्यायेन जीवाम्यहम् ।।

A traveller reached a town and enquires from a Brahmin, "O Brahmin, who is the greatest in this town?" Brahmin replied, "The toddy trees."

The traveller asked again, "Who is the great giver here?"

The answer was, "The washerman! He collects the clothes for washing or dying in the mornings and gives them back in the evenings."

The traveller wanted to know, "Who's clever around here?"

"All men of this town are clever in stealing the money and wives of others," the Brahmin replied.

"Then, how do you survive in this place?" The traveller wondered.

The Brahmin said, "I am like a worm who takes birth in filth, lives in filth and dies in filth. Poisonous filth. I am living like that." (8)

The first of the question and the answer needs explanation. To the query about the great or tall the replies is 'The toddy trees.' The toddy trees secrete toddy which is a milky intoxicant. The locals drink it to get drunk. The meaning of the answer was that no one was great or tall. All the men were drunkards who failed to stand on their legs even. That left only the toddy trees standing tall. The men were mostly in the gutters.

विप्रपादोदककर्दमानि
न वेदशास्त्रध्वनिगर्जितानि ।
स्वाहा-स्वधाकार-विवर्जितानि
श्मशानतुल्यानि गृहाणि तानि ।।

A house is a cremation ground where the feet of the Brahmins is not washed making the floor muddy, where the holy scriptures are not read out to echo in the rooms, where yajna is not performed and worship is not done. (9)

Guru Chanakya shows his orthodox dogmatic face again.

सत्यं माता पिता ज्ञानं धर्मो भ्राता दया स्वसा।
शान्तिः पत्नी क्षमा पुत्रः षडेते मम बान्धवाः।।

A common man asks from a saint who sits in a divinely blessed mood about his family. The saint replies, giving introduction of his family, "Truth is my mother, Knowledge is my sire, Religion is my brother, Mercy is my sister, Peace is my wife and Tolerance is my son. All these six make my family." (10)

अनित्यानि शरीराणि विभवो नैव शाश्वतः।
नित्यं सन्निहितो मृत्युः कर्तव्यो धर्मसंग्रहः।।

This body does not last forever, the wealth does not stay at one place, the death is always hovering around. So, everyone must live riligiously and engaged in good deeds. (11)

आमन्त्रणोत्सवा विप्रा गावो नवतृणोत्सवाः।
पत्युत्साहयुता नार्यः अहं कृष्णरणोत्सवः।।

For a Brahmin the invitation for meals is the festival, finding a green pasture is a festival for a cow, improving virility of a husband is a festival for his woman and faith in God is my festival. (12)

Finding such good couplet is a festival for a thoughtful reader. We hope you are the one.

मातृवत् परदारांश्च परद्रव्याणि लोष्ठवत्।
आत्मवत् सर्वभूतानि यः पश्यति स पश्यति।।

A person who sees mother in the woman of another man, who values the wealth of others nothing more than rubbish and who sees his own soul in all the other creatures is really the one who has found the truth. (13)

Such a persons should infact be the one who has achieved the unification with God. Because he has crossed all the frontiers that separate us from God. He has won the last of all the battles of self-realisation and made God proud for creating him.

धर्मे तत्परता मुखे मधुरता दाने समुत्साहता
मित्रेऽवञ्चकता गुरौ विनयता चित्तेऽति गम्भीरता।
आचारे शुचिता गुणे रसिकता शास्त्रेषु विज्ञानता
रूपे सुन्दरता शिवे भजनता सत्स्वेव संदृश्यते।।

Only the noble souls reveal the qualities of; ever being religious, speaking polite words, keenness for charity, complete faith in a sincere friend, humility towards the guru, serene nature, pious behaviour, being receptive to the good advices, having the knowledge of the scriptures and faith in Creator. (14)

काष्ठं कल्पतरुः सुमेरुरचलश्चिन्तामणिः प्रस्तरः
सूर्यस्तीव्रकरः शशी क्षयकरः क्षारो हि वारांनिधिः।
कामो नष्टतनुर्बलिदितिसुतो नित्यं पशुः कामगौ—
नैतांस्ते तुलयामि भो रघुपते कस्योपमा दीयते।।

O Lord Rama, who do I compare you with? Kalpavriksha tree has power to grant wishes but it is merely wood. Sumeru is mighty but it is just a mountain. Chintamani frees one from all worries but it it's only a gem. The sun is brilliant but it is roasting hot, the moon is beautiful but its beauty keeps decreasing or increasing. The sea is deep but its water is saline. The cupid is handsome but it has no physical existence and king Bali is extremely kind but he is of demonic breed. Kamadhenu is all providing but it is only a cow. You are indeed incomparable. (15)

Kamadhenu, Kalpavriksha, Sumeru, Chaintamani gem and King Bali are items, creatures or characters, quoted from mythological literature.

विनयं राजपुत्रेभ्यः पण्डितेभ्यः सुभाषितम् ।
अनृतं द्यूतकारेभ्यः स्त्रीभ्यः शिक्षेत् कैतवम् ।।

A learner can learn lessons or arts from any one. Learn; politeness from princes or other royal persons, endearing words from scholars, bluff from gamblers and the cunningness from women. (16)

अनालोक्य व्ययं कर्ता ह्यनाथः कलहप्रियः ।
आतुरः सर्वक्षेत्रेषु नरः शीघ्रं विनश्यति ।।

The destruction of following persons is certain; who overspends due to having no foresight to budget his expenditure, who is physically weak but has tendency to pick up quarrels and who is desirous of having affairs with all kinds of women. (17)

नाहारं चिन्तयेत् प्राज्ञो धर्ममेकं हि चिन्तयेत् ।
आहारो हि मनुष्याणां जन्मना सह जायते ।।

A wise person must not worry about his food, the source of the next meal. Just go on doing your religious duties. It is God who arranges for everyone's food. (18)

Sometimes the couplets appear to be contradictory to one another. One couplet advises hardwork and planning in every sphere of life and the very next preaches just the opposite. It is believed that many such couplets are addition to the sets of the original couplets. The Hindu scriptures suffer from this sort of adulterations which corrodes their value greatly.

जलबिन्दुनिपातेन   क्रमशः पूर्यते घटः।
स हेतुः सर्वविद्यानां धर्मस्य च धनस्य च।।

Drop by drop a pitcher gets filled. Similarly, a little by little collection of money. Learning and good works become great treasures. (19)

वयसः परिणामेऽपि यः खलः खल एव सः।
सुपक्वमपि माधुर्यं नोपयातीन्द्रवारुणम्।।

A person who is evil by nature does not become good even after gaining maturity. Similarly, as a bitter pumpkin does not mellow into sweetness even after becoming overripe. (20)

The Summary of the Chapter

Chanakya has again extolled the virtues of the obedient sons and daughters, sweet talking faithful wife, earning by honesty, sincere friends, loving and caring father and man and being religious dutifully.

There is an interesting exchange between a traveller and a resident Brahmin of a town of drunkards, money grabbers, wife stealers and uncharitable characters. The life in such place has been likened to the life of worm who takes birth, lives and dies in a rotting mass of filth.

In other couplet Chanakya laments and puts a curse on one who does not do any work of charity, who has not gone on any pilgrimage, who has not lent ears to recitations of holy books and discourses by the holymen and who has amassed wealth by dishonest means.

A man who is not jealous and not desirous of another man's money, who does not have evil designs on the women of others and who has same feelings for all the creatures as he has for himself, is the one who is the nearest to God.

At one place Chanakya advised the things to learn from others which includes gamblers and women. From gamblers he wants us to learn bluffing, an art of keeping up straight face to protect the secrecy of one's own hand. And women have been acknowledged for having the qualification to impart the art of subterfuge and cunning tricks.

❏❏

CHAPTER THIRTEEN

Strange is the character of noble souls. They don't give much weight to the importance of riches yet when riches comes to them the weight of the money bends them down into more humility.

मुहूर्तमपि जीवेच्च नरः शुक्लेन कर्मणा।
न कल्पमपि कष्टेन लोकद्वयविरोधिना।।

If a man were to live the life of mere three quarters of an hour, he should live it doing good turns. But, in any world, a life of thousands of years, spent in committing sins is worthless. (1)

Longevity of a life is not important. It is the deeds done during a life time that matter. Far better is to have a small green garden than own a hundreds of kilometres of desert. Don't waste your life any more.

गते शोको न कर्तव्यो भविष्यं नैव चिन्तयेत्।
वर्तमानेन कालेन प्रवर्तन्ते विचक्षणाः।।

Let the bygones not worry you. And don't fear the future.

The wise ones concentrate on making good use of the present. (2)

If the present is spent in doing good deeds, it automatically brightens up the future prospects because the future is nothing but the consequence of the present. And past is past which is beyond repair or change.

स्वभावेन हि तुष्यन्ति देवाः सत्पुरुषाः पिता ।
ज्ञातयः स्नानपानाभ्यां वाक्यदानेन पण्डिताः ।।

The wise, the gentlemen and the father are by nature content, the kith and kin are pleased with good food and the learned ones take only a few polite words to get satisfied. (3)

अहो बत विचित्राणि चरितानि महाऽऽत्मनाम् ।
लक्ष्मीं तृणाय मन्यन्ते तद्भारेण नमन्ति च ।।

Strange is the character of noble souls. They don't give much weight to the importance of the riches yet when riches comes to them the weight of the money bends them down into more humility. (4)

Money makes the cheap characters vainful and arrogant. They boast and flaunt their money in a very ugly way which earns the contempt of others. But the money has just the oppsotie effect on the noble people. More riches makes them more polite and more gentle to the pleasure of everyone.

यस्य स्नेहो भयं तस्य स्नेहो दुःखस्य भाजनम् ।
स्नेहमूलानि दुःखानि तानि त्यक्त्वा वसेत्सुखम् ।।

One who is infatuated with someone or something faces a threat from the same someone or something. Because it has become his weakness. It breeds a host of problems and worries. Give up infatuation if you want to be happy and in control of yourself. (5)

अनागतविधाता च प्रत्युत्पन्नमतिस्तथा ।
द्वावेतौ सुखमेधेते यद्भविष्यो विनश्यति ।।

One who prepares oneself to meet the impending danger saves himself suceessfully and tides over any problem. He is happy. But the one who leaves everything to fate thinking that whatever will be, will be, gets perished. (6)

Here is exactly what we have been contending. In clear terms Chanakya is advising not to be foolish by depending on fate which would certainly prove disastrous. He exhorts us to prepare ourselves to face the percieved problem or danger. In an earlier couplet he was shown adivising everyone to leave things to the fate stating that whatever is written in fate was bound to happen. The human effort was of no consequence. How can a scholar like Chanakya say such ridiculously cotradictory things. Hence, it is clear that the parts propagating fatalism and the greatness of Brahmins are not Chanakya's thoughts. They are dubious thoughts inserted with dishonest intentions by some vested interests made up of orthodox Brahmins. Such elements have not even spared Geeta. What a pity!

राज्ञि धर्मिणि धर्मिष्ठाः पापे पापाः समे समाः ।
राजानमनुवर्तन्ते यथा राजा तथा प्रजाः ।।

If the King is religious and pious, the subjects would be of similar nature. If the King is sinful then the subjects would hcve no hesitation in committing sins. If the King is careless the subjects too will care for nothing. As the King is, so will be the subjects.(7)

In the middle ages the masses saw in their Kings the role models. Hence, the King being upright was need for the upliftment of the whole population.

जीवन्तं मृतवन्मन्ये देहिनं धर्मवर्जितम् ।
मृतो धर्मेण संयुक्तो दीर्घजीवी न संशयः ।।

A man without religion is a living dead. A man with religion lives even after the death.(8)

A man with religion will do some good deeds memories of which will survive his death on this earth. And in the another world he will be honoured with the life in the heaven.

धर्मार्थकाममोक्षाणां यस्यैकोऽपि न विद्यते ।
अजागलस्तनस्येव तस्य जन्म निरर्थकम् ।।

A man who has no religion, no riches, no love and no hope of salvation in death, the life of such a man is as ridiculous as udders in the neck of a goat.(9)

दह्यमानाः सुतीव्रेण नीचाः पर-यशोऽग्निना ।
अशक्तास्तत्पदं गन्तुं ततो निन्दां प्रकुर्वते ।।

The low people burn in jealousy of the people who have achieved the success and earned the glory. They themselves achieve nothing but find some consolation is belittling the achievers.(10)

बन्धाय विषयाऽऽसक्तं मुक्त्यै निर्विषयं मनः ।
मन एवं मनुष्याणां कारणं बन्धमोक्षयोः ।।

देहाभिमाने गलिते विज्ञाते परमात्मनि ।
यत्र यत्र मनो याति तत्र तत्र समाधयः ।।

A man is merely states of mind. In one state of mind, he finds himself trapped in the worldly desires. A shift in the state of mind can free him of all the trappings.(12)

A man's life is only a result of his thought processes. The thought's implemented are good deeds or bad acts. When a person's mind decides to set itself on the course of the spiritual awakening the person is redeemed.

ईप्सितं मनसः सर्वं कस्य सम्पद्यते सुखम्।
दैवाऽऽयत्तं यतः सर्वं तस्मात्सन्तोषमाश्रयेत्।।

All the desires are impossible to fulfil. The fate can't grant all of them and the efforts fall short. The best alternative is to learn and be content with what one gets.(13)

यथा धेनुसहस्रेषु वत्सो गच्छति मातरम्।
तथा यच्च कृतं कर्म कर्तारमनुगच्छति।।

In a herd of thousands of cows, a calf unerringly locates its mother easily. Similarly, the consequences of a person's actions follow him without any let up.(14)

अनवस्थितकार्यस्य न जने न वने सुखम्।
जने दहति संसर्गो वने सङ्गविवर्जनम्।।

A disorganised person is comfortable neither in society nor in jungle. In the society the rebukes and the criticism of others annoy him. And in Jungle, the loneliness troubles him and drives him crazy.(15)

A man without any rules or methods faces failure everywhere. He is a total misfit in all situations.

यथा खात्वा खनित्रेण भूतले वारि विन्दति।
तथा गुरुगतां विद्यां शुश्रूषुरधिगच्छति।।

Digging the earth gets one the water. In the same way serving the guru yields him the knowledge. (16)

In ancient times the teacher was the sole source of knowledge or learning and there was no written literature or other aids available to students. The lessons were mostly passed on by the teacher orally to his students. And naturally a student who pleased his teacher more got more valuable tips accordingly. There are numerous instances where famed teachers imparted some special knowledge only to their favoured students denying same to the other pupil of their classes.

कर्मायत्तं फलं पुंसां बुद्धिः कर्मानुसारिणी।
तथापि सुधियश्चाऽऽर्याः सुविचार्यैव कुर्वते।।

A man gets rewards according to his deeds and the mind also works programmed to it. This knowledge does not deter the wise and the noble from giving a careful thought to any deed they begin.(17)

एकाक्षरप्रदातारं यो गुरुं नाभिवन्दति।
श्वानयोनिशतं भुक्त्वा चाण्डालेष्वभिजायते।।

One who does not worship God and does not pay obeisance to Him, takes hunderd births in dog life and then is born to the family of a charlatan. (18)

The talk of dog's life and Charlatan family is figurative merely to illustrate the badness of the act of not having faith in God.

युगान्ते प्रचलते मेरुः कल्पान्ते सप्त सागराः।
साधवः प्रतिपन्नार्थान् न चलन्ति कदाचन।।

After the end of an era the Sumeru mountain too gets dislodged and after an epoch the seas deluge the land by crossing its shore limits. But a superior man remains firm on his resolve to fulfil the promise given. (19)

The Summary of the Chapter

A short stay in heaven is far better then a long tenure in the hell. A small patch of green land is worth having compared to large tract of desert land. Quality of possession is more important than quantity of it. The life must be spent in doing good deeds of quality.

A man must prepare to face the impending dangers or hardships to successfully meet the challenges when they come. Only after an adequate preparation for war an invader can be beaten back. The people who did not do this became the slaves of others or got destroyed or swept away by the events. To leave things to fate is utterly foolish and a cowardly act. In several other couplets Chanakya has been shown to advise the inaction and dependence on fate. It raises the doubts about the genuineness of several couplets or quatrains accepted as part of *Chanakya Neeti*. There is definite ground to believe that many of them are fake and additions by some vested interests who wanted Hindus to remain slaves to the dogmas of a particular priestly caste.

A King or any other kind of ruler is required to be a person of good qualities because it has been observed that the masses take him for their role model. If a King is a bad character then the people of his Kingdom will generally be of bad character.

A man must have some achievement to his credit to account for his life. Either be a man of learning, or religiously impeccable, or a man of wealth or a success in love or be a good family man doing his duties as father, son and husband. Otherwise the life is a wasted one.

❏❏

CHAPTER FOURTEEN

O man! If you want to win this world with just one act, then don't let your tongue speak ill of any other person. That is it.

पृथिव्यां त्रीणि रत्नानि जलमन्नं सुभाषितम् ।
मूढैः पाषाणखण्डेषु रत्नसंज्ञा विधीयते ।।

This earth is blessed with only three real gems; Water, food grains and the words of good wish. But the fools think that the precious stones are gems.(1)

आत्माऽपराधवृक्षस्य फलान्येतानि देहिनाम् ।
दारिद्र्यरोगदुःखानि बन्धनव्यसनानि च ।।

Poverty, deseases, problems, pains and bandages; these are all fruits of the man's own tree of misdeeds.(2)

पुनर्वित्तं पुनर्मित्रं पुनर्भार्या पुनर्मही ।
एतत्सर्वं पुनर्लभ्यं न शरीरं पुनः पुनः ।।

Money lost can be regained, friends can be made and a new wife can be had through a remarriage. But a human body is not renewable.(3)

बहूनां चैव सत्त्वानां समवायो रिपुञ्जयः ।
वर्षधाराधरो मेघस्तृणैरपि निवार्यते ।।

Unity is strength. People can come together to make an army and vanquish the enemy. Similarly, as straws unite to become a thatch to serve as a roof of a structure and provide safety from the rain.(4)

जले तैलं खले गुह्यं पात्रे दानं मनागपि ।
प्राज्ञे शास्त्रं स्वयं याति विस्तारं वस्तुशक्तितः ।।

The oil or water, secret with a bad character, donation to a worthy recipient and learning of a wise one; all these have a natural property to spread over.(5)

Put a drop of oil on water and it spreads over a wide surface into a thin film. Tell secret to a person of bad character and he will whisper it into thousand ears to spread it, a worthy recepient of a donation or a grant will sing praises of the generosity of the donor, earning him good name all around. And the learing of wise one will spread to others as he will try to impart the knowledge to everyone coming into his contact.

धर्माऽऽख्याने श्मशाने च रोगिणां या मतिर्भवेत् ।
सा सर्वदैव तिष्ठेच्चेत् को न मुच्येत बन्धनात् ।।

The awakening aroused in mind at the occasions of; hearing of sermons or religious discourses, attending a funeral in the cremation ground and illness; if were to remain alive, a man would certainly achieve his final salvation.(6)

In the situations cited in the couplet one does find oneself at a new spiritual level, far above the mundane matters of life. One becomes aware of God beyond and a yearning for spiritual liberation sweeps the mind. A certain detachment from the carnal existence develops. But this strange mindset quickly evaporates when one relapses into his normal life and daily chores.

उत्पन्नपश्चात्तापस्य बुद्धिर्भवति यादृशी।
तादृशी यदि पूर्वं स्यात् कस्य न स्यान्महोदयः॥

A man repents after committing a sin. If the same wisdom were to be there before the commission of the sin instead of being a hindsight, man would become a certain candidate for Nirvana, as he would shun the sins.(7)

दाने तपसि शौर्ये वा विज्ञाने विनये नये।
विस्मयो न हि कर्तव्यो बहुरत्ना वसुन्धरा॥

A man must not become vain upon doing charity, penance, gaining knowledge, cultivating politeness and on becoming worldly wise. Because this world is full of gems who excel in these fields and are far more accomplished. There is always one better.(8)

दूरस्थोऽपि न दूरस्थो यो यस्य मनसि स्थितः।
यो यस्य हृदये नास्ति समीपस्थोऽपि दूरतः॥

The one who lives in someone's heart is by one's side even if physically the one may be at a far off place. But the one who is not in heart, who is not dear, is distances away, even if the one may be sitting next physically.(9)

The nearness of a person depends upon the emotional relationship. The physical positioning is not important. It's all really a matter of the heart.

यस्य चाप्रियमिच्छेत् तस्य ब्रूयात् सदा प्रियम्।
व्याधो मृगवधं कर्तुं गीतं गायति सुस्वरम्॥

One whom you want to harm should be treated to a

sweet enticement to make him lower the guard or to deceive him. Similarly as a hunter minics the call of an animal that he is hunting for.(10)

अत्यासन्ना विनाशाय दूरस्था न फलप्रदाः ।
सेवितव्यं मध्यभागेन राजा वह्निर्गुरुः स्त्रियः ।।

Do not stay too close to; the King, the fire and the women. It's dangerous. But do not stay too far off them. It will gain you no rewards. Just keep hovering around at a safe distance.(11)

The above three are useful to a person. One badly needs them. The King gives rewards, employment and opportunites. But he is a dangerous person, a creature of moods and whims who can do fatal damage if he gets angered. Hence, a distance is a must for the safety from his foul moods. But be near enough to take advantage of his benevolent phases. And women too are similarly finicky minded.

A woman can spell doom or bless one with love, the greatest gift of God to a man. A woman is a man's dearest need. Hence, don't stay too close to get blown away by her ire. But stay near about to be blessed with the pleasures. And in case of fire, being too near it will burn, a safe distance and it will provide warmth besides cooking all the delicacies of the world.

अग्निरापः स्त्रियो मूर्खाः सर्पा राजकुलानि च ।
नित्यं यत्नेन सेव्यानि सद्यः प्राणहराणि षट् ।।

The fire, water, women, fool, snake and the royal family; beware of all these. They can prove fatal.(12)

स जीवति गुणा यस्य यस्य धर्मः स जीवति ।
गुणधर्मविहीनस्य जीवितं निष्प्रयोजनम् ।।

Only a man of religion and qualities survives in the real sense in this world. A man devoid of these lives a life of no purpose.(13)

यदीच्छसि वशीकर्तुं जगदेकेन कर्मणा।
परापवादसस्येभ्यो गां चरन्तीं निवारय।।

O man! If you want to win this world with just one act, then don't let your tongue speak ill of any other person. That is it.(14)

प्रस्तावसदृशं वाक्यं प्रभावसदृशं प्रियम्।
आत्मशक्तिसमं कोपं यो जानाति स पण्डितः।।

A real wise man is who; knows to talk according to the situation, speaks in a manner befiting his fame and grace and shows anger according to his power to handle the consequences. (15)

In this couplet the advice to moderate one's anger to suit one's power is significant. If one displays anger at the mightier opponent than one is then shall face disaster. It might lead to one's ruin. Hence, the control over anger is very important to justify it and to see to it that it does not bring any harm or humiliation.

एक एवं पदार्थस्तु त्रिधा भवति वीक्षितः।
कुणपः कामिनी मांसं योगिभिः कामिभिः श्वभिः।।

An object is viewed by three different Characters in three ways. An ascetic views a beautiful woman as nothing more than a corpse. The woman is an object of desire for a lustful man. And for a dog she is merely a lump of meat.(16)

सुसिद्धमौषधं धर्मं गृहच्छिद्रं च मैथुनम्।
कुभुक्तं कुश्रुतं चैव मतिमान्न प्रकाशयेत्।।

A wise man must not reveal anything about; formula of one's private medicine, one's own religious resolves, family blemish, sexual acts, bad food taken and the ill talk heard. (17)

In bygone age everyone was free to concoct any medicine and to try to on any willing person. The professionals too had their own concoctions as medicines. Sometimes some professional could come up with a good one. So, it was good for his business to keep the formula of the medicine a secret. The religious resolves were not revealed because the enemies used to defile the holy sites of rituals which required to be performed according to strict procedures and piety. The sexual acts must not be reported because it betrays the confidence of the sex partner. The bad food taken hints at one's indiscriminate nature which lowers one's honour in the eyes of the others. Relaying ill talk unwittingly makes one a back biter, a very bad character.

तावन्मौनेन नीयन्ते कोकिलैश्चैव वासराः ।
यावत्सर्वजनानन्ददायिनी   वाक्प्रवर्तते ।।

Until the arrival of the spring, the cuckoo does not give its call. She remains quiet and sings only when the spring sets in which makes her the heralder of the bloom.(18)

Things done at the right time are greatly appreciated.

धर्मं धनं च धान्यं च गुरोर्वचनमौषधम् ।
सुगृहीतं च कर्तव्यमन्यथा तु न जीवति ।।

For a well-planned and organised life one must; live religiously, earn money and save, store food grains, keep life saving and first aid medicines in domestic stock and act upon the advice of the teacher.(19)

त्यज दुर्जनसंसर्गं भज साधुसमागमम् ।
कुरु पुण्यमहोरात्रं स्मर नित्यमनित्यताम् ।।

O man, give up the company of the evil people, go to the fold of the noble ones, do good deeds every day and night and remember God because the world will perish one day. (20)

The Summary of the Chapter

There are only three real gems in this world which sustain our life; the water, the foodgrains and the learning. The precious stones are no gems because the life does not depend on them. If a person who is marooned on an island with no inhabitation were to be asked to choose three things from a long list of things he would opt for the above three and leave out precious stones. Because the above three are so basic to life. You can't drink pearls, you can't eat diamonds and the rupies can't satisfy the mind's hunger for knowledge. The sweet words of good wishes is infact the manifestation of an educated mind and its wisdom.

The unity is strength. Through unity impossible can be made possible. The guile and the craftiness is also a powerful weapon. It can lure the enemy just like the hunter's trick of minicking the call of the prey does.

One should be extremely careful about dealing with the people in power and women. They are creatures of shifting moods. Stay too near to them and some day harm will come. But don't go too far away from them because they are exteremely useful. They have the capacity to reward you with riches, honour and the great pleasures.

One should not become egoistic because of some achievement because there always is one better in this world in any field of activity, Don't give up politeness and humility.

One must moderate one's anger according to the situation. It should be kept in mind that the backlash of the act of anger should be manageable. Otherwise the result can be destructive. You can well imagine that what will happen if a dog dares to lose anger at a tiger. Similarly, one should know what to say in which situation. And always speak with dignity.

The people see things according to their state of mind. For an ascetic a woman can just be a walking corpse. For a draper she is something wrapped in a fine dress and for a horse she is just a burden.

The oil on water, a secret with a loose tongue, a charity to a grateful person and the learning of a scholar have the natural tendency to spread over. A secret with a loose tongued evil person gets told to everyone. It no more remains a secret just like a drop of oil on the water does not remain a drop. It becomes a thin film spread over a wide area. A scholar spreads around the knowledge he has.

Out of sight is not always out of mind. Infact a dear one who is out of sight can be right there in mind. The distance of the separation is a matter of heart. A person who is not dear means distances away though he may be sitting just nearby.

The best single act is not to speak ill of others.

❑ ❑

CHAPTER FIFTEEN

A man loses woman, friends, relatives and servants when he loses the money. When the money is regained they all come back. Hence, the money is a man's real relative.

यस्य चित्तं द्रवीभूतं कृपया सर्वजन्तुषु।
तस्य ज्ञानेन मोक्षेण किं जटाभस्मलेपनैः ।।

A man whose heart gets moved with compassion for all the creatures, does he need any religious signs to be displayed to become religious?(1)

The mercy and compassion are the mothers of all the religions.

एकमेवाक्षरं यस्तु गुरुः शिष्यं प्रबोधयेत्।
पृथिव्यां नास्ति तद्द्रव्यं यद्दत्त्वा चाऽनृणी भवेत् ।।

A teacher who introduces his disciple to God, leaves an unpayable debt on his pupil. For, there is no enough precious thing or enough amount of money that can pay this debt.(2)

खलानां कण्टकानां च द्विविधैव प्रतिक्रिया ।
उपानन्मुखभङ्गो वा दूरतो वा विसर्जनम् ।।

There are only two ways of dealing with the evil
persons or thorns; Crush them under your boot or stay far
away from them.(3)

कुचैलिनं दन्तमलोपसृष्टं
बह्वाशिनं निष्ठुरभाषिणं च ।
सूर्योदये चास्तमिते शयानं
विमुञ्चति श्रीर्यदि चक्रपाणिः ।।

One who; wears dirty clothes, keeps his teeth filthy, is
glutton, speaks foul language and oversleeps; gets ignored
by the prosperity, health, beauty and grace. Even God can't
afford the above shortcoming.(4)

Here a pleasant fact emerges that guru Chanakya was
very conscious about teeth. He understood the importance of
keeping the teeth clean by regular brushing. The teeth are
vital factor in building up one's total personality. Clean teeth
provide grace to the words spoken by a person. Things of
even great importance and wisdom spoken remain
unconvicing if they come through the filth of the unclean
teeth. It is as simple a fact as the desirability of a delicacy to
be served in a clean plate. A delightful dish in a dirty bowl
spoils the taste.

It was generally believed that natives of India were
ignorant about the basic matters of hygiene. But Chanakya
knew all about it, as proved by this couplet.

त्यजन्ति मित्राणि धनैर्विहीनं
दाराश्च भृत्याश्च सुहृज्जनाश्च ।
तं चार्थवन्तं पुनराश्रयन्ते
अर्थो हि लोके पुरुषस्य बन्धुः ।।

A man loses woman, friends, relatives and servants when he loses his money. When the money is regained they all come back. Hence, the money is a man's true relative.(5)

अन्यायोपार्जितं द्रव्यं दश वर्षाणि तिष्ठति ।
प्राप्ते चैकादशे वर्षे समूलं तद् विनश्यति ।।

The money earned by unjust means remains only for ten years, at the most. In the very beginning of the eleventh year it perishes, all of it, the capital and the gains, everything. (6)

It is difficult to explain this kind of exact calculation which has no basis, formula or table and mathematical logic. May be, this idea has been picked up from some mythological story which is not very well-known. Anyway, the message is that ill gotten money does no good. Sooner or later it will go as easily as it has come.

अयुक्तं स्वामिनो युक्तं युक्तं नीचस्य दूषणम् ।
अमृतं राहवे मृत्युर्विषं शङ्करभूषणम् ।।

Even an incorrect act done by men of power and authority gets justified and hailed. And even a correct deed done by a person of low birth gets criticised and condemned on various counts. The demon Rahu lost his life when he partook nectar. But Lord Shiva gulped down the deadliest of the poisons and became immortally more adored. His apple turned blue by the effect of the poison became his distinguishing mark and a symbol of his greatness.(7)

तद्भोजनं यद् द्विजभुक्तशेषं
तत्सौहृदं यत्क्रियते परस्मिन् ।
सा प्राज्ञता या न करोति पापं
दम्भं विना यः क्रियते स धर्मः ।।

The real food is that which is left over after a Brahmin has taken his meals. The real love is one which is showered on the strangers. And the real religious act is one which does not breed vanity as a by-product.(8)

In the first advice of this couplet Chanakya appears to be batting for his cast again. And in the process the people of other castes don't get the benefit of the shower of his love.

मणिर्लुण्ठति पादाग्रे काचः शिरसि धार्यते।
क्रयविक्रयवेलायां काचः काचो मणिर्मणिः।।

A gem might be adorned by the foot as part of an ornament and a glass object might get a place on a head but that does not change their values. While trading, the gem will command its value and the glass will get poor value.(9)

अनन्तशास्त्रं बहुलाश्च विद्याः
अल्पश्च कालो बहुविघ्नता च।
यत्सारभूतं तदुपासनीयं
हंसो यथा क्षीरमिवाम्बुमध्यात्।।

The holy scriptures like Vedas are seas of vast knowledge. And the knowledge itself is spread over countless fields and subjects. But human life is very short and full of hurdles. Hence, only the gist of the knowledge should be sought. Just like a swan that sips the milk and leaves out water.(10)

It is a mythological belief that the swans have the skill of separating milk from the water.

दूरागतं पथि श्रान्तं वृथा च गृहमागतम्।
अनर्चयित्वा यो भुङ्क्ते स वै चाण्डाल उच्यते।।

If a weary, dead tired and hungry traveller stumbles in

to a home, after a long journey, hoping for some food and rest, but the home owner does not care to welcome the guest and show inhospitality, sits down to take his own meal ignoring the guest, such a man certainly is a real charlatan of meanest order.(11)

पठन्ति चतुरो वेदान् धर्मशास्त्राण्यनेकशः।
आत्मानं नैव जानन्ति दर्वी पाकरसं यथा।।

Devoid of the soul of the knowledge are those who study all the great scriptures and treatises but learn nothing about the soul and God. They are like a ladle that goes through all kinds of delicious dishes but never knows what taste is.(12)

It is more like the dogmatic Brahmins who recite all the scriptures and read them so many times that they learn and can remember the mantras or couplets or quatrains by heart. They can sing them without having to consult the scriptures or books. But most of the Brahmins never know or don't care to know the meaning and importance of what they recite.

धन्या द्विजमयी नौका विपरीता भवार्णवे।
तरन्त्यधोगताः सर्वे उपरिस्थाः पतन्त्यधः।।

In this world, which is sea of woes, Brahmin serves as a boat. The boat has strange nature. The ones who live low in it get safely transported but who arrogantly try to mount it get tossed into the sea. Hail the boat. (13)

The message is that others should remain and serve at the feet of Brahmins meekly. Anyone who dares to play arrogant and does not pay respect to the Brahmins will pay a heavy price. The bottom line is that the other Hindu castes must humbly feed Brahmins, serenade them and treat them as virtual gods.

अयममृतनिधानं नायकोऽप्यौषधीनां

अमृतमयशरीरः कान्तियुक्तोऽपि चन्द्रः ।

भवति विगतरश्मिर्मण्डलं प्राप्य भानोः

परसदननिविष्टः को लघुत्वं न याति ।।

Frequenting the homes of others corrodes one's respect in these families. Just as the case of moon is. It is considered to be a store of the nectar, It is god of medicines, Its soothing rays are like divine balm and it has glow. But the same moon when appears in the home of the sun i.e. in day time, it gets reduced to a mere pale shadow.(14)

अलिरयं नलिनीदलमध्यगः कमलिनीमकरन्दमदालसः ।

विधिवशात्परदेशमुपागतः कुटजपुष्परसं बहु मन्यते ।।

The black bee sits amidst the petals of lotus enjoying to nectar. It is a heavenly situation. But it does not stay put and wanders off to paddy fields and jungles to taste the honey of alien flowers getting pierced by their thorns.(15)

The lure of the foreign lands is irresistible. One gets rarely satisfied with whatever the homeland has to offer and sails off, though the venture is perilous and full of risks.

पीतः क्रुद्धेन तातश्चरणतलहतो वल्लभो येन रोषाद्

आबाल्यादद्विप्रवर्यैः स्ववदनविवरे धार्यते वैरिणी मे ।

गेहं मे छेदयन्ति प्रतिदिवसमुमाकान्तपूजानिमित्तं

तस्मात्खिन्ना सदाहं द्विजकुलनिलयं नाथ युक्तं त्यजामि ।।

Lord Vishnu puts a question to his better half, Laxmi, the goddess of prosperity, "Why do you disfavour Brahmins?" She replies, "Agastya Rishi, gulped down the sea in anger. The sea, my father. Brahmin Bhrigu, in rage, stamped his foot on the chest of my husband, Vishnu. These Brahmins are always partial to my rival Saraswati, the goddess of learning. They plunder my garden to steal away lotus flowers to use as the offering to Lord Shiva in worship. My Lord, these are the reasons why I don't favour Brahmins."(16)

The incidents referred to in the dialogues of Laxmi are from some mythological episodes. Chanakya appears to be drawing consolation for the poverty of Brahmins by rationalising the fact in above manner. The poor financial state of Brahmins always pained him.

बन्धनानि खलु सन्ति बहूनि प्रेमरज्जुदृढबन्धनमन्यत् ।
दारुभेदनिपुणोऽपि षडंघ्रिर्निष्क्रियो भवति पङ्कजकोशे ।।

There are many types of bondages in this world. But the bondage of love is unique. It is paralysing. The black bee has the power to bore holes in wood. But the same bee remains trapped in the petals of lotus unable to bore its way to freedom because it is in love with the flower. In deep love.(17)

छिन्नोऽपि चन्दनतरुर्न जहाति गन्धं
वृद्धोऽपि वारणपतिर्न जहाति लीलाम् ।
यन्त्रार्पितो मधुरतां न जहाति चेक्षुः
क्षीणोऽपि न त्यजति शीलगुणान् कुलीनः ।।

Sandalwood does not stop being fragrant even if it is chopped to pieces. The bull elephant does not stop mating even in old age. The cane does not lose sweetness even when crushed or extruded. Similarly a man of class does not stop being a gentleman even in poverty. (18)

The Summary of the Chapter

Compassion is the holiest of all the religions and the most glorious act. A person with mercy and compassion is himself a living religion. He does not need any label, any symbol, any certificate, any uniform, any physical sign and any recommendation to be called a religious person. The act of compassion is itself a prayer to God. Evil persons and thorns deserve to be crushed under the shoes.

Cleanliness is next to Godliness. A person who puts on unwashed clothes, keeps his teeth dirty, speaks foul things and is addicted to laziness, becomes a poor wretch. His health deteriorates. The people shun such a character. No one likes to be on good terms with him and be respectful to him.

Money is the real relative of a man because it creates all other relatives. And it must be seen that money is earned by just and honest means. The money amassed through dishonesty gives little pleasure and it is counter productive. Life of Brahmins is miserable because they fail to understand the value of money. Learning is no substitute to it. For an intellectual exercise is dependent on physical existence. And only money makes the physical existence viable and possible. It makes one powerful. Even a good deed done by a person of no power gets no recognition. The money and power can justify even the wrong acts.

This world is a vast sea of knowledge. It is not possible for a person to imbibe all the knowledge because human life is very short. So, one must selectively choose the knowledge according to his needs or plans. The best way is to know the gist of the general knowledge of other fields.

One should not frequent the homes of others to safeguard his respect in the eyes of the others. The love and respect shown to the strangers is the real ones. Because every one loves his own near and dear ones. It is as simple as one eating food or drinking water. The generosity is when one offers food to the hungry and water to the thirsty whom he does not even know. Even a stranger who by sheer chance stumbles into your house, he should be accorded full honours reserved for a guest of honour. That is when a person rises above the normal level and redeems his soul.

❏ ❏

CHAPTER SIXTEEN

This world is a tree that bears different kinds of evil and bitter fruits. It produces only two sweet fruits, polite words and the company of the saintly people.

न ध्यातं पदमीश्वरस्य विधिवत्संसारविच्छित्तये
स्वर्गद्वारकपाटपाटनपटुर्धर्मोऽपि नोपार्जितः ।
नारीपीनपयोधरोरुयुगलं स्वप्नेऽपि नालिङ्गितं
मातुः केवलमेव यौवनवनच्छेदे कुठारा वयम् ।।

A man who has not remembered God to free himself from the dragnet of the carnal world, who has not collected the wealth of religion to open the doors of the heaven, who has not even in dreams enjoyed the pleasures of a woman's beautiful breasts and the juicy thighs; such a man is like an axe that cuts down the forest of the mother's youth that created him.(1)

If you have taken birth, do something, achieve something to redeem your life. Do not insult your mother's youthful energy that so lovingly gave you life to see her future dreams of purposeful actions reflected in it.

जल्पन्ति सार्धमन्येन पश्यन्त्यन्यं सविभ्रमाः।
हृदये चिन्तयन्त्यन्यं न स्त्रीणामेकतो रतिः॥

The whores don't love one man. A whore talks with a man, but she keeps ogling at another man and her mind has thoughts of a third man. An utter fool is a man who thinks that a certain whore is in love with him.(2)

यो मोहान्मन्यते मूढो रक्तेयं मयि कामिनी।
स तस्य वशगो भूत्वा नृत्येत् क्रीडा-शकुन्तवत्॥

A foolish man who thinks that a certain whore love him, becomes a toy in her hands. She uses him, deceives him, plays devious games with him and fleeces him.(3)

कोऽर्थान् प्राप्य न गर्वितो विषयिणः कस्यापदोऽस्तं गताः
स्त्रीभिः कस्य न खण्डितं भुवि मनः को नाम राज्ञां प्रियः।
कः कालस्य न गोचरत्वमगमत्कोऽर्थी गतो गौरवं
को वा दुर्जनवागुरासु पतितः क्षेमेण यातः पथि॥

There is no man in this world who didn't develop ego upon gaining riches and living a life of luxury. There is no one who did not get troubles upon indulging in worldly desires. There is no one who did not fall for some beauteous woman. Which beggar has ever got respect of others? And who has escaped unscathed after getting involved with evil people?(4)

न निर्मितः केन न दृष्टपूर्वः न श्रूयते हेममयः कुरङ्गः।
तथाऽपि तृष्णा रघुनन्दनस्य विनाशकाले विपरीतबुद्धिः॥

A golden dear has never been created and no one ever saw such a thing. Yet, Lord Rama got realy to get a golden deer for his beloved wife, Sita. It is clear that in adverse times a man's wisdom deserts him.(5)

गुणैरुत्तमतां याति नोच्चैरासनसंस्थिताः ।
प्रासादशिखरस्थोऽपि काकः किं गरुडायते ।।

A man achieves the heights by dint of his good works and qualities. A crow perched on a steeple of a royal palace does not become an honourable bird.(6)

गुणाः सर्वत्र पूज्यन्ते न महत्योऽपि सम्पदः ।
पूर्णेन्दु किं तथा वन्द्यो निष्कलङ्को यथा कृशः ।।

Everywhere a man is respected on account of his qualities. No respect accrues to a person of no qualities even if he has loads of money. A little bright moon of the second day of ascendence is worshipped more than the full moon.(7)

Moon of the second day of ascendence is held a great respect in Hindu religion. There are several religious rites related to it and festival's celebrated on this night of moon. This moon phase is considered more pious than any other day of moon.

पर-प्रोक्तगुणो यस्तु निर्गुणोऽपि गुणी भवेत् ।
इन्द्रोऽपि लघुतां याति स्वयं प्रख्यापितैर्गुणैः ।।

A man who is praised by others inspite of his being a man of no qualities, gets the fame and the glory. But if Lord Indra himself sang his own praise it will only look a lowly act. Selfpraise earns no one's respect.(8)

विवेकिनमनुप्राप्ता गुणा यान्ति मनोज्ञताम् ।
सुतरां रत्नमाभाति चामीकरनियोजितम् ।।

Just as a gem studded in gold ornament looks more graceful, a man must stud his personality with qualities to enhance its beauty.(9)

गुणैः सर्वज्ञतुल्योऽपि सीदत्येको निराश्रयः ।
अनर्घ्यमपि माणिक्यं हेमाश्रयमपेक्षते ।।

A greatly learned person of high qualities can be in a sad state if he does not find a good patron. A highly valued diamond also prays for a gold ornament to be studded in.(10)

Even today persons of skill and art need sponsors to get ahead professionally. In middle ages it was more true and important. There was no marketing system to sell the works of the man of art and craft. The only stages for display learning, art, music or dance were the courts of Kings or chambers or gardens of rich merchants. So, an artist or a scholar badly needed a patron to survive and earn fame.

अतिक्लेशेन ये चार्था धर्मस्यातिक्रमेण तु ।
शत्रूणां प्रणिपातेन ते ह्यर्था मा भवन्तु मे ।।

I don't want the money earned by; Exploiting others, causing pain to others, working against the interests of the religion and begging before the enemy.(11)

किं तया क्रियते लक्ष्म्या या वधूरिव केवला ।
या तु वेश्येव सा मान्या पथिकैरपि भुज्यते ।।

Money which is like bride of an orthodox family meant for the use of only one man is no good. The money is good if it is like a prostitute available to everyone who wants it.(12)

The money locked up in a richman's safe is a dead capital which serves little purpose except providing pleasure to its greedy owner. The money should be available to all deserving people who have good projects to execute for general welfare and the public good.

धनेषु जीवितव्येषु स्त्रीषु चाहारकर्मसु ।
अतृप्ताः प्राणिनः सर्वे याता यास्यन्ति यान्ति च ।।

*There is no man in the world who is completely satisfied
with; the amount of money he has got, the pleasures he got
from women and the varieties of food he has savoured. The
more you get these things the more you desire for. It is a
hunger that never gets satisfied and the thirst that never gets
quenched.(13)*

क्षीयन्ते सर्वदानानि यज्ञहोमबलिक्रियाः ।
न क्षीयते पात्रदानमभयं सर्वदेहिनाम् ।।

*The blessings earned through donations of land, clothes,
water and food or by performing yajna or other religious
rites or sacrificial offerings; all of it can be nullified. But the
credit earned through help to the deserving needy and the
mercy shown to any creature is irrevocable.(14)*

तृणं लघु तृणात्तूलं तूलादपि च याचकः ।
वायुना किं न नीतोऽसौ मामयं याचयिष्यति ।।

*In this world, a straw is extremely light. Cotton is still
lighter. But a begger is the lightest of them all. So, why
doesn't the wind blow him away like a straw or a cotton
puff? May be, the wind is scared that the beggar might seek
alms from it.(15)*

It is Chanakya's satirical way of ridiculing the act of
begging. And it shows how lightly he thinks of the beggars.

वरं प्राणपरित्यागो मानभङ्गेन जीवनात् ।
प्राणत्यागे क्षणं दुःखं मानभङ्गे दिने दिने ।।

*It is better to die than live the life of humiliation. Death
kills once only but one dies everyday in life of dishonour.(16)*

प्रियवाक्यप्रदानेन सर्वे तुष्यन्ति जन्तवः।
तस्मात्तदेव वक्तव्यं वचने का दरिद्रता।।

Everyone gets endeared by a polite talker. One should speak sweetly. It costs nothing. So, why be miser with sweet words?(17)

संसारविषवृक्षस्य द्वे फले अमृतोपमे।
सुभाषितं च सुस्वादु सङ्गतिः सुजने जने।।

This world is a tree that bears different kinds of evil and bitter fruits. It produces only two sweet fruits, the polite words and the company of the saintly people.(18)

जन्म-जन्मन्यभ्यस्तं दानमध्ययनं तपः।
तेनैवाऽभ्यासयोगेन तदेवाभ्यस्यते पुनः।।

A man does the noble deeds of charity, learning and penance in one life and then repeats them in other life times through rebirths. This process becomes an exercise and doing above deeds becomes a habit.(19)

Doing good deeds just needs a beginning. Once begun, the goodness of it inspires repetitions and sets a soul on the road to salvation.

पुस्तकेषु च या विद्या परहस्तेषु यद्धनम्।
उत्पन्नेषु च कार्येषु न सा विद्या न तद्धनम्।।

The knowledge which is in the books and the money which is with others is of no use. In the hour of need such knowledge and money doesn't help. (20)

The real knowledge is one which has been transferred from the books to one's mind, properly imbibed. And the real money is what one has on him, properly earned.

The Summary of the Chapter

The life is to be made use of. It should not be wasted in doing nothing. One should try for salvation through penance and noble deeds. Such good deeds generate so much good feeling that they inspire one to repeat the act. The exercise continues through the next lives to become a habit which will eventually unite one with the Creator. If one is not inclined to redeem the life spiritually, realise some carnal dreams at least. Get the happiness of love and romance. Enjoy the beauty of woman and ravish their juicy bodies. Or get rich and live the life of luxury. Buy all pleasures the money can buy. Have the satisfaction of having done someting with life. Not doing anything will be a shame for your mother who so lovingly brought into this world her unspelled dreams in your shape with a fond hope that you will turn out to be a beautiful gift package of actions.

Good qualities of a person embellish his personality like gems give beauty to a gold ornament. And a telented person needs a patron to survive and get appreciated just like a diamond needs a crown or an ornament to glitter.

The money is best when it is like a prostitute, available to all who have good ideas to invest it. The money which lies in a safe of a rich man unused is wrothless as far as the society is concerned. It is a dead capital.

The most insignificant existence is that of a beggar. Even the work insignificant is more significant than him. And a straw and a cotton puff carry more weight than him.

The polite words don't cost anything. Don't be miser with them. Infact, they will earn you rich love of others. More you spend them, richer you will get. The meaningful knowledge is what you have learnt and the meaningful money is what you have got in your pocket.

❑❑

CHPATER SEVENTEEN

A snake's venom is in its fangs. A bee's poison is in its sting. A scorpion's poison is in its tail. But there is poison in every part of the body of an evil person.

पुस्तकप्रत्ययाधीतं नाधीतं गुरुसन्निधौ ।
सभामध्ये न शोभन्ते जारगर्भा इव स्त्रियः ।।

The knowledge merely copied from books and which is not properly imparted by a teacher is bastard knowledge. It is as illegitimate as a child conceived by a woman from a man other than her husband. Such knowledge is never recognised by any faculty of scholars, the same way as a bastard is not respected in the society.(1)

Today there is no harm in learning from the books because well produced authentic books on every subject are available in the market. Many a hobbies a person learns solely from the books. But generally a teacher is required to provide proper guidance and clarifications on whatever point is needed.

A few centuries ago the situation was very different when Chanakya penned down his thought. The printing was not yet invented. The books were prepared in hand-writing which used to be full of mistakes. Even such books were difficult to find. Every copier considered it his birth right to add something of his own to the original matter. There was no check on it. Many times deliberate additions were made with malafide intentions to mislead the reader. Most of the religious scriptures carry such dubious insertions making it difficult to sift out the authentic matter. This book itself is an perfect example of this. As we have already pointed out that many couplets or quatrains look completely out of place in this collection. They stand out like asses would in a troop of horses. As the collection has been traditionally accepted we can't delete the suspect matter. We can just alert the reader wherever we consider it necessary.

Thus, trying to gain knowledge from dubious copies was always risky.

कृते प्रतिकृतं कुर्याद् हिंसने प्रतिहिंसनम् ।
तत्र दोषो न पतति दुष्टे दुष्टं समाचरेत् ।।

There is no sin in dealing with persons in quid-pro-quo manner. Deal out gratefulness to the grateful, violence to violent one and evil to evil character.(2)

यद्दूरं यद्दुराराध्यं यच्च दूरे व्यवस्थितम् ।
तत्सर्वं तपसा साध्यं तपो हि दुरतिक्रमम् ।।

Something which looks too far off to achieve, intangible and too high to attain, can be reached through persevearance, dogged effort, hard work and single minded devotion. Nothing is impossible. Even God is just a true penance away.(3)

लोभश्चेदगुणेन किं पिशुनता यद्यस्ति किं पातकैः
सत्यं चेत्तपसा च किं शुचि मनो यद्यस्ति तीर्थेन किम् ।

सौजन्यं यदि किं गुणैः सुमहिमा यद्यस्ति किं मण्डनैः
सद्विद्या यदि किं धनैरपयशो यद्यस्ति किं मृत्युना।।

If a man is infested with greed, he needs no other evils.
If a man is a back-biter, can there be a bigger sinner? If he
is truthful and of good character, does he need to do any
penance or meditation? If a man's heart is pious why should
he go on pilgrimage? If a man knows to love others, does he
require any other quality? If a person is earning fame does
he need any ornament to add to his beauty? And if a man
has knowledge, does he need wealth to feel rich? (4)

पिता रत्नाकरो यस्य लक्ष्मीर्यस्य सहोदरा।
शङ्खो भिक्षाटनं कुर्यान्नाऽदत्तमुपतिष्ठते।।

The conch shell is a product of sea. Goddess Laxmi too
was born out of the sea. So, she is a sister of the conch shell.
The mendicants seek alms by blowing the conch shell
making it an instrument of begging. But Laxmi is greatly
respected for being the goddess of prosperity. Hence, origin
is not important. It is the deeds which earn one good name
or notoriety. (5)

अशक्तस्तु भवेत्साधुर्ब्रह्मचारी च निर्धनः।
व्याधिष्ठो देवभक्तश्च वृद्धा नारी पतिव्रता।।

Sometimes helplessness forces good characteristics on
people. A physically weak person develops friendly nature
because he can't afford to be tough. Similarly a poor person
becomes symbol of morality because women and luxuries
are out of his reach. A sick man becomes devotee of God.
And an old lady becomes a woman of virtues because she
can no more play a naughty girl. (6)

नाऽन्नोदकसमं दानं न तिथिर्द्वादशी समा।
न गायत्राः परो मन्त्रो न मातुः परं दैवतम्।।

No charity is greater then giving foodgrains and water.
No date is more pious then twelveth of the month. No
mantra is greater than Gayatri mantra. No deity is greater
than the mother.(7)

The twelveth of the month is considered most pious by
Hindus. The good deeds done on this date are believed to earn
greater credit than other days. Many religious rites are
performed on this day. This date has special mention in
mythological stories too.

तक्षकस्य विषं दन्ते मक्षिकायास्तु मस्तके।
वृश्चिकस्य विषं पुच्छे सर्वाङ्गे दुर्जने विषम्।।

The venom of a snake is in its fangs. The poison of a bee
is in its sting. The poison of a scorpion is in its tail. But there
is poison in every part of the body of an evil person.(8)

पत्युराज्ञां विना नारी उपोष्य व्रतचारिणी।
आयुष्यं हरते भर्तुः सा नारी नरकं व्रजेत्।।

A woman who keeps fast without permission of her
husband shortens the life of the husband. She goes to hell
and is punished with great horrors of the hell.(9)

No modern educated person must support this kind of
view. Infact, woman baiting had been favourite passtime of
ancient scholars and the common men injected with worst
gender bias. This trait of the scholars of ancient world makes
even their wisdom and learning suspect.

न दानैः शुध्यते नारी नोपवासशतैरपि।
न तीर्थसेवया तद्वद् भर्तुः पादोदकैर्यथा।।

No amount of charity can salvage a woman. No amount of fasting can cleanse her. No prilgrimage can redeem her. Her only hope is in serving at the feet of her husband.(10)

Please read the preceding comment again.

दानेन पाणिर्न तु कङ्कणेन
स्नानेन शुद्धिर्न तु चन्दनेन।
मानेन तृप्तिर्न तु भोजनेन
ज्ञानेन मुक्तिर्न तु मण्डनेन॥

The charity is the beauty of the hands, not bangles or other wrist ornaments. The body gets cleansed by a bath, not by application of sandalwood paste on the forehead. The real satisfaction comes from honour, not from food. The learning is the salvation of life, not the rituals.(11)

नापितस्य गृहे क्षौरं पाषाणे गन्धलेपनम्।
आत्मरूपं जले पश्यन् शक्रस्यापि श्रियं हरेत्॥

The utter disgrace is; to go to the barber's shop for a shave, application of sandalwood paste on stone, or application of scent and looking at one's own reflection in the water. These acts can bring unmitigated disaster.(12)

These appear to be some irrational, orthodox and outdated beliefs steeped in blind faiths. It is strange that Chanakya too believed in them.

सद्यः प्रज्ञाहरा तुण्डी सद्यः प्रज्ञाकरी वचा।
सद्यः शक्तिहरा नारी सद्यः शक्तिकरं पयः॥

Eating of kundroo vegetable destroys one's brain in no time. Vacha herb repairs the damage and improves the power of the brain. Sex with women saps a man's energy. Milk restores the lost energy.(13)

Another set of outdated theories and beliefs.

परोपकरणं येषां जागर्ति हृदये सताम् ।
नश्यन्ति विपदस्तेषां सम्पदः स्युः पदे पदे ।।

Those people whose heart's have warmed up to the desire of doing good for others get blessed with riches at every step and their troubles get blown away.(14)

आहारनिद्राभयमैथुनंच सामान्यमेतत् पशुभिर्नराणाम् ।
धर्मोऽहितेषामधिको विशेषो धर्मेण हीनाः पशुभिः समानाः ।।

Humans and animals are alike in the acts of; eating, sleeping, displaying fear and mating. The only thing that is special to humans is religion. Hence, a man without religion is like a beast.(15)

दानार्थिनो मधुकरा यदि कर्णतालैर्
दूरीकृताः करिवरेण मदान्धबुद्ध्या ।
तस्यैव गण्डयुगमण्डनहानिरेषा
भृङ्गाः पुनर्विकचपद्मवने वसन्ति ।।

Black bees sit on the forehead of an elephant to partake the nectar that oozes out of the Jumbo's cheeks in the mating season. But the crazed fool of an elephant scares the bees away by flapping its ears. The bees lose nothing. They go and sit on the lotus flower which offers them nectar. The loser is the elephant itself. Because the bees sitting on the elephant's forehead were creating the impression of a crown giving it a graceful look.(16)

राजा वेश्या यमो ह्याग्निस्तस्करो बालयाचकौ ।
परदुःखं न जानन्ति अष्टमो ग्रामकण्टकः ।।

The following are very callous; a King, prostitute, fire, The god of death, thief, child, beggar and the tormentor of villagers. They don't understand the pain of others.(17)

The tormentors of villagers could be feudal agents or the men of the King. They heartlessly collected revenues or took away the grains as the feudal Lord's share without caring for the hunger and poverty of the villagers. The hardships they faced due to floods or famines aroused no sympathy in the agents who were examples of heartlessness.

अधः पश्यसि किं वृद्धे पतितं तव किं भुवि।
रे रे मूर्ख न जानासि गतं तारुण्यमौक्तिकम्।।

An extremely old women who walked by with bent back appearing to be looking down for something was asked by a youth sarcastically. "Ancient lady, what for do you look down? Lost something or dropped something down there?"

The old woman replied, "Fool! Don't you know that the pearl of my youth years is lost? I look for the same."(18)

Only the old people know what it really means to be young. It is the most precious stage of one's life. The full realisation of its value dawns only when it's gone.

व्यालाश्रया ऽपि विफलाऽपि सकण्टकाऽपि।
वक्राऽपि पङ्किल-भवाऽपि दुरासदाऽपि।
गन्धेन बन्धुरसि केतकि सर्वजन्तोर्
एको गुणः खलु निहन्ति समस्तदोषान्।।

O Pandanus tree! The snakes keep slithering over you. You don't bear any fruit. You grow thorns instead. You stand in mud. No fragrance emanates from you. You are difficult to locate. But still your peculiar smell charms everyone. How strange! (19)

One good quality in a person redeems his life and helps cover up other shortcomings. Similarly as the learning of Chanakya gave him a beautiful honour, fame and respect of others. No one minded his ugly face.

The Summary of the Chapter

Chanakya propagated the principle of eye for an eye or violence for violence. Some great people differ on this issue. Mahatma Gandhi believed otherwise. He was in favour of meeting violence with non-violence and very successfully demonstrated it.

The real knowledge it what is imparted by a proper teacher. Bookish knowledge is inferior and incomplete.

In this chapter, Chanakya has said some very irrational and uncharitable things about women which can not be accepted by a modern mind. His thoughts are based on prejudice, gender bias and orthodox beliefs born of blind faiths. It is a great pity that sclolar like Chanakya surrendered his wisdom before woman baiters.

There is nothing in this world that can not be achieved through hard work and perseverance. Even God is only a true penance away.

Greed is root cause of all evils. And capacity to love is the best of all the qualities a good character can have. Truthfulness is the best penance.

Sometimes people adopt good qualities by default. A physically weak person displays extremely polite and gentle behaviour because he can't afford to be hostile. A poor person becomes moralistic because he has no money to buy luxuries or indulge in merry making. An old woman becomes paragon of virtue when the days of romancing and playing naughty are well over.

One exceptionally good quality in a person covers up all the minor faults and failings.

A Treasure of Stories

Specially for CHILDREN

Big Size Illustrated